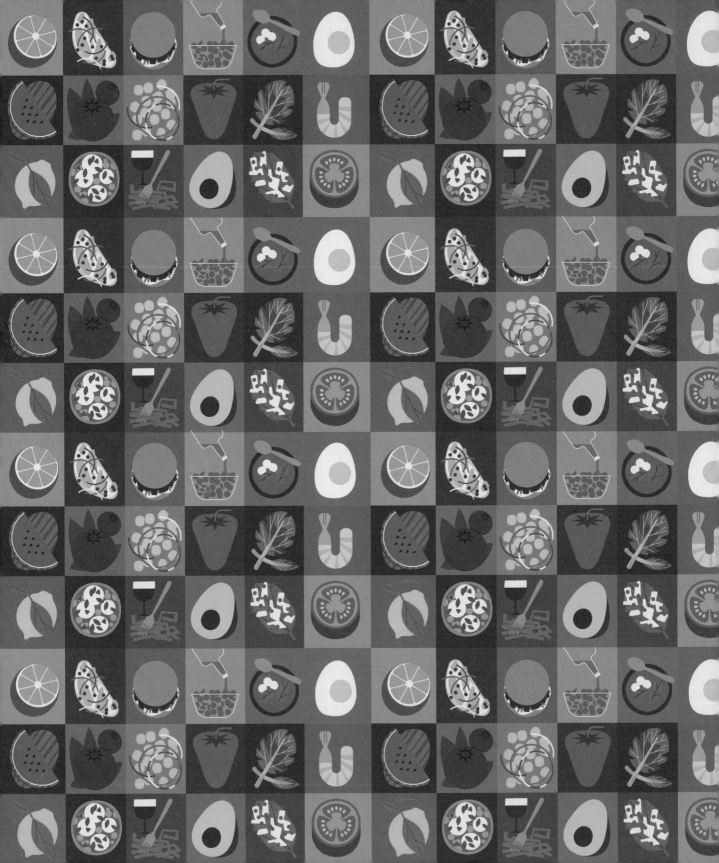

AMONG THE POTS AND PANS

ALEX EARLY

HARVEST HOUSE PUBLISHERS
EUGENE, OREGON

For Jana, Tovah, and Jude.
I am happiest when
I'm with you.

CONTENTS

PRESENCE

I'm a pastor who loves to cook. So, I'll begin with a confession: I have no more business preaching in a pulpit than I do cooking in a kitchen, but that's how grace works—we happily get to belong in an undeserved place. Grace is not something you "say" at dinnertime. Grace is first received, then passed out like warm bread rolls around the table of your life. The beloved preacher and novelist Frederick Buechner said, "Grace is something you can never get but can only be given. There's no way to earn it or deserve it or bring it about any more than you can deserve the taste of raspberries and cream or earn good looks or bring about your own birth."[1] A great responsibility is plopped into the lap of those who understand that they are a thick slab of butter melting smack-dab in the middle of the pancakes of God's love. Yes! A responsibility to show up and *live*!

Though we haven't met, I'm sure we have more in common than just a love of cooking. We're human and that means that we don't just enjoy the sweetness of grapes at weddings, caramel sundaes with our kids, and baklava with our friends; common humanity has also served up undercooked bitter greens and flat tap water. Upon finishing college and getting married, I, like so many of my peers, launched out into marriage and ministry with an absolutely profound naivete, one worth sharing in a book such as this. I had some theology on tap, charisma baked into my personality, and newly adorned rose-colored glasses. I set sail only to strike more than one iceberg, and the icebergs were brutal. I've had my heart shattered in ways from which I thought I'd never recover. In 2015, the *SS Early* began taking on water, and without making some drastic changes, our marriage, faith, and our very selves were soon to be lost at the bottom of the sea. So we slowed down, took a hiatus from ministry for over a year to work on our marriage and minds. Jana and I went to good marriage counseling and individual therapy and homed in on things in our past that were affecting our present and would ultimately ruin the future. Yes, your mental health matters. Counseling is good for you. If you think you need some help, just go. There's no more shame in going to therapy than in going to your dentist or chiropractor or taking Tylenol for a headache. Go and be made well. Your future self will thank you immensely.

The most profound wisdom you'll collect throughout life is often found near tremendous loss, grief, and gnawing disorientation. Next time you're on a hike in the forest, take note—a fern is usually close to poison ivy. Lesson: the medicine is usually near the poison. One of my best friends, Mikey, was also going through a terrible season of life at the same time. He and I would ride around in Atlanta listening to Big Sean, Future, and T.I., and stay up late cooking, crying, and talking. One night, after listening to *The Life of Pablo*, Mikey said, "Alex, we gotta turn this pit into a laboratory. Make sure you're taking some notes while you're down there in your pit. I know I am." I'm glad I listened to Mikey. Though I'm far from perfect, I want to be a good steward of my pain, and much of that stewardship is reflected in the pages of this beautiful cookbook. This cookbook is about relational wealth, the gentleness of Jesus of Nazareth, living and dying in a state of gratitude, and being faithfully present in this world as a whole human being. Essentially, I'm dining on the raspberries and cream known as the gospel. Oh, and there's a seat open next to me.

Presence in the Kitchen

The cry of God's heart down through the centuries right up to this very moment has been for men and women to dare to believe that God will embrace us as we are—and not the version of ourselves that we think he wants to see—to dare to risk it all and to cast our lives, our souls, our stories, everything (even our kitchen sinks) into the hands of he who is Present, Holy, Love. Speaking of the kitchen, how did you get into cooking? Did you grow up with a parent or grandparent showing you the way around the heart of the home? What are some of your memories in the grocery, hovering over the stove, or dicing onions? Who is there with you in the kitchen? I grew up in Woodstock, Georgia, where my mom, Bevy, did all the cooking. We were a right-down-the-middle kind of rural family, eating really simple foods: taco casserole, meatloaf, and steak cooked to the consistency of a tractor tire. It was simple, functional, and time-sensitive dining. Yet every last meal was, as they say, "made with love."

I began cooking around the same time that I began pastoring. If it weren't for my friend Jon, I would've maybe missed out on my favorite way to spend time: in the kitchen with music playing, a glass of wine sitting, family laughing, and friends embracing. Jon helped me see that I desperately needed to work creatively with my *hands*. Most of my life is made of words—reading words, writing words, speaking words, and most importantly, *listening* to words. I spend a lot of time with people, and I spend a lot of time in my study with my books (or, as Bevy calls them, my "friends"). My first week in the parish taught me something important about my occupational work: nothing really feels "finished." You might also relate, for this nagging feeling of incompletion is a common trait for workers in nearly every occupation. Whether you're a stay-at-home parent or a Fortune 500 company CEO, *more* could always be accomplished. One more load of laundry, a little more fine-tuning to a spreadsheet, one more meeting. However, we're not machines; we're human beings. The myth of "more" leaves us as dull as butter knives. It's frustrating, to say the least. You and I are far more needy than we want to admit, and one of those needs is the simple satisfaction of knowing that a task is completed.

As a pastor, I immediately saw that people are never *finished*, especially me. We're all a work in progress, from when we arrive until the day we depart this life. Similarly, sermons are never finished. There is no reaching the bottom of the depth of the Word of God. So how do I begin to say the words of God to the people of God who have been entrusted to me as I have been entrusted to them? How do I carry the stories of God and the people, and even my own story, to completion? How do I say all that is true, kind, and beautiful? Nothing in my work as a pastor is ever *finished*. So I wanted to complete creative work with my hands. Should I golf? Pastors seem to like golf. That sounds nice, I guess, but that would take me away from my wife, Jana, and the kids for hours, and missing out on family isn't one of our priorities. Life moves too quickly, and then too slowly, and I want to be present with my family. Really, really *present*. What about painting? I like to paint, but when I do, I'm all alone. What about playing music? I suppose I could start a band, but unless it's going to be the Early Family Grunge Band, count me out.

Cooking, though . . . *Cooking* would provide a place to get creative *and* bring everyone together. The kitchen is where everyone winds up anyway. Sometimes, while cooking, my friends or family jump in and dice some cilantro, julienne carrots, or roll out pizza dough. As they do so, we talk, laugh, and spend time discussing a particular cooking technique, soccer practice, work, or whatever. The topic doesn't matter, because when you're among friends, there's no such thing as "small talk." You're just there, present, together; you're happy. Georgetown philosophy professor James Schall noted, "We know that the only time worth having is the time we waste on our friends. And our prayer is the time we 'waste' with God, the time we take to comprehend all that is given to us, *all that is.*"[2] James is right. Whoever we waste our time with is who we love.

Presence in the Community

Cooking is about so much more than being in my kitchen for hours. In this way, it is similar to Sunday worship: liturgy begins long before the Call to Worship; it begins with the previous week's benediction. The liturgy of the dining experience begins at the grocery store, a place I go every day without fail. Here in Seattle, we're blessed with phenomenal groceries everywhere. The one I frequent is called Town & Country.

Those who earn a living in supermarkets and food stores are some of the hardest working people in the world, and their labors can't be overlooked or taken for granted. They're on their feet constantly, stocking shelves, doing inventory, and answering questions about where the preserved lemons are kept, when fresh corn will be available again, and how early to request specific cuts of meat around the holidays. Everyone in the city goes to the grocery and speaks with these blessed, shelf-stocking, question-answering, produce-bagging saints. Most of the time, the questions asked of them have to do with groceries. But it's not uncommon to hear customers and clerks catching up for a moment by the cheese counter or wine cabinet: "How's your dad? You mentioned he was sick. I've been thinking about you"—which is how grocery store friends say, "I love you."

My grandmother (MaMa, pronounced "Muh-Mah") also knew everyone in her grocery. She would notoriously play pranks and give nicknames to those undeserving Publix employees. They loved her! Somehow I followed in her footsteps, though I haven't started pranking them (yet). During the 2020 pandemic, the grocery was often the only place anyone could (or *would*) go here in Seattle. We got to know each other not just by name but by making eye contact. Upon walking in, I could see my masked friends smiling at me through their squinting eyes. That meant a lot to me.

From the cheese- and fishmongers to the butchers, produce managers, and cashiers . . . we're friends. My friend Grace will shout when I walk in, "Hey, preacher! Hop in my line when it's time to check out!" She loves to point out all my tattoos to others in line and playfully pick on me, asking either the person bagging the groceries or the next customer behind me, "Guess what kind of work he does?" The answer is always the same: artist or musician. And then Grace laughingly responds, "He's a *pastor*! Can you believe that?" I'll usually go along with the joke and say, "Apparently, God will take anybody." Evan is a manager; he and I talk about music we love. My friend Erin will kindly remind me that I'll be sorry if I don't run back and grab cabbage for my dumplings. I know she's right. I love the grocery, and I love my friends there even more. In a way, this cookbook is an expression of appreciation for them.

This book, however, is not only about cooking. The photos are not only about aesthetics. The recipes are not only about conquering hunger or even engaging your palate. Of course, those things are a given in any cookbook, but they're not really what this one is about. Instead, this is about *showing up* to the one life you've been given, practicing being present, and finding all your wealth in your relationships.

You don't need an advanced degree in culinary arts to enjoy freshly baked bread or a PhD in theology to savor the "bread that came down from heaven" (John 6:51 NIV). In fact, you already have what you need: you have your life. And now is the time to show up to it. It's time to show up to God and all that he is with all that you are (and all that you are not). It's time to courageously attend to your own soul and story. It's time to notice, love, and cherish the friends and family around you. After all, they're not supporting actors in the drama of your life; they *are* your life.

Pause. Before you read another sentence, take a sip of coffee, water, or wine, take a deep belly breath—seven seconds in and a slow exhale—and then proceed. Ready? Here it is: if you don't show up and live your life, nobody else will. What is more tragic than absence? The word we use for the Great Tragedy is *death*. When someone we love dies, there's always an empty chair at the table, and the surviving loved ones feel their absence profoundly. Why live half-present? Why should anyone go about aimless, distracted, and absent?

What happens if *you* miss *your* life? Answer: you will die two deaths. An absent life is the death before "Death." But presence is life before "Life." For those of us who belong to Jesus, we live in the in-between; we are made new and currently await the King's return in which all will shine like brand-new stainless steel pots and pans. So hear the wake-up call! As long as there's breath in your lungs, there's life to be lived! Hear the ear-piercing kettle-cry of the Bible: for the love of God, show up. Out of respect for yourself, show up. And for the betterment of humanity, show up. Please. We need you. The dinner party of our life isn't complete without you. There's no good reason to dillydally, drag your feet, or delay on your one go at this gift of life.

Now, showing up is a lot harder than it sounds. Maybe you know what I'm talking about. The average person checks their phone 344 times throughout the day.[3] We're spending an inordinate amount of time staring down at these screens. Sometimes we're working, and it's necessary; other times, we're just distracted, seeking little hits of dopamine, and are met with feelings of missing out, insecurity, jealousy, and anxiety. Meanwhile, *life is happening all around us*. A spouse, child, friend, or neighbor could benefit from our simple decision to be present. You deserve peace of mind, too, you know? The solution for most of us is not throwing our phones into the sea, abandoning society, and starting a modern ascetic movement. Instead, we must face the challenge of *stewarding* our technology, time, and relationships like never before. It's challenging but not impossible. The trick is to see the challenge not as a stripping away of joy but as an invitation into what the Bible calls holiness.

Holiness has less to do with stained glass, choirs, and an orderly Sunday morning liturgy and more to do with being uniquely present to God while living moment by moment. Time, like pastries, can suddenly be filled with the holy custard of God's presence. The only thing required is your attention to that ongoing reality. Whether it's me barefoot in Seattle before my gas stove or Moses barefoot before the burning bush of Horeb, ground becomes holy when our attention is on the dancing flame of God.

Presence at the Table

This holiness I'm talking about is nothing new. Saints like San Pasqual, Brother Lawrence, and Teresa of Avila have long found the kitchen, with its ordinary tasks, the place of deep spiritual and communal formation. San Pasqual was born in Spain during the feast of Pentecost (Pascua de Pentecosta) in 1540. As a monk, he served the poor more than a bowl of broth; he served them bread and meat because they deserved to be humanized, treated like everyone else. He said, "I joyfully celebrate the food I am given. May it deeply nourish everyone that I feed." San Pasqual knew that a table is more than furniture; it's holy space where people are nourished and known. At the table, we practice being present and we become wholly human. As we dip bacon-encrusted cornbread into bowls of chili, we talk, laugh, question, answer, and listen. We can do our best learning, thinking, and growing at the table.

On one occasion, Teresa told her students that "God walks among the pots and pans." She grasped the reality that every single place, every table—from the communion table to your picnic table—is holy if we will only become present to the God who already *is*.

The daily routines of sharpening knives, caring for our ingredients, and maintaining our tools are all ways we mystic-chefs enjoy God and guacamole. Intentionally looking after the kitchen is not pointless, tedious work. It is where we are changed. In her award-winning book *Liturgy of the Ordinary* (which sports a peanut butter and jelly sandwich on the cover), Tish Warren writes, "We are not left like Sisyphus, cursed by the gods to a life of meaninglessness, repeating the same pointless task for eternity. Instead, these small bits of our day are profoundly meaningful because they are the site of our worship. The crucible of our formation is in the monotony of our daily routines."[4]

Yes, with our hands submerged in the soapy warm water, scrubbing pots and pans, God is present. As we put our plates back into the cupboard for tomorrow, God is present. As we turn out the lights and close the kitchen for the evening, God is present, calling us to rest.

I'm glad you're here.
Let's waste some time together.

1

FOOD IN THE BIBLE:
Meals Are Stories

The body of Christ was broken for you. The blood of Christ was shed for you.[1] Bread has been torn, dipped into wine, and given to humble, grateful sinners-made-saints for thousands of years. As we have chewed, swallowed, and digested that simple meal, the magnificent story of God has been *metabolizing* in our stomachs, minds, and souls all around the globe. Of the ten thousand graces I have received, one of the most special happens to be my friend Brian McDonald. Brian's a world-class storyteller. His mind and heart are what companies like Pixar lean on for insight into story structure, armature, cohesion, and consistency. Brian *insists* that the purpose of a story is not to be cute, unique, or even entertaining. The purpose of a story is to tell the truth in a way that imparts survival information. For

example, in *The Three Little Pigs*, the survival information essentially says, "Don't play while you're supposed to be working. When you work, work wisely; build your house with bricks, not straw or sticks."

The Bible is the story of God and the lifeblood of his children. In writing his story, God spoke through more than Moses with his stone tablets, Jeremiah with his papyrus, Jesus on the mountainside, and apostles in synagogues, marketplaces, and house churches. He chose the farm, grocery store, and pantry. He thought of fruit, vegetables, meat, salt, corn, wheat, barley, water, milk, honey, bread, wine, fish, oil, grapes, dill, cumin, and locusts. He told his story through seeds sprouting, wheat being harvested, grain being ground, yeast rising, the stove baking, and friends dining. Feasts of tears and joy make up the life of faith around the table of God. From cover to cover of Scripture, food is used to tell both God's story and our own.

Eden

In the opening pages of Scripture, we read of God's good design as he created humans in his image, yet needy, dependent, and hungry. Adam and Eve would require daily food and drink and rest to sustain life. The ongoing graces of growing, gathering, preparing, and dining would make up the human experience. Ample provisions were made, but not everything in sight was to be brought to the table. Some things were to be left as they were. "You may surely eat of every tree of the garden, but of the tree of the knowledge of good and evil you shall not eat, for in the day that you eat of it you shall surely die" (Genesis 2:16-17). Life and death hung in the balance of the diet. Only eight verses later, the serpent famously asked (and continues to ask!), "Did God actually say, 'You shall not eat of any tree in the garden'?" (Genesis 3:1). Did you hear him correctly? Are you sure? Look around at this place. Certainly, God's not being stingy with you! Or maybe he is? And as the story goes, Eve soon bought the lie, took the fruit, gave it to Adam, and they dined in rebellion.

Sin, shame, guilt, fear, hiding, and death entered God's good creation. Therefore, if there was to be any redemption, any hope, any kind of saving grace, it would not come from those who had fallen into the pit; forgiveness, salvation, and the healing of our relationships must come from God himself. And thus, food is not only present in our downfall, but food would also be used to tell the story of the grace of God.

Egypt

The second book of the Bible tells the story of the mighty Exodus of the people of God. The infamous night of the Passover was introduced as the great rescue of God got underway, and the Jewish people still celebrate this beautiful holiday every year all over the globe. We'll explore this more in chapter 2.

Zion

In the eighth century BC, the prophet Isaiah was sent to proclaim a message of judgment and salvation to the people of God, a message of famine and feast. While being held accountable for sin, the people of God received the promise that famine would not be the final word. Isaiah went to Jerusalem, stood on Mount Zion, and painted a picture that transcends time and language, inviting every culture from around the world.

> On this mountain the LORD of hosts will make for all peoples a feast of rich food, a feast of well-aged wine, of rich food full of marrow, of aged wine well refined. And he will swallow up on this mountain the covering that is cast over all peoples, the veil that is spread over all nations. He will swallow up death forever; and the Lord GOD will wipe away tears from all faces, and the reproach of his people he will take away from all the earth, for the LORD has spoken (Isaiah 25:6-8).

What a beautiful day we long for! Aged wine, choicest meats, a rich and savory feast, and as we raise our glass to the King and swallow heaven's finest cooking, God will "swallow up death forever." The death blow to death itself was delivered through Christ himself. The *story* continues . . .

Christ

Seven hundred years after the prophecy of Isaiah, the story of God continued when the very "Word became flesh and dwelt among us" (John 1:14). Jesus Christ was born in the city of Bethlehem to Mary and Joseph, simple people. He grew up in the humble community of Nazareth. Nazareth is never mentioned in the Old Testament; the Jewish historian Josephus never makes mention of the town, nor does any of the rabbinic literature, such as the Mishnah or Talmud, comment on Nazareth. Nevertheless, the small and insignificant town, numbering between approximately 200 and 400 people[2], caused Nathanael to ask Philip, "Can anything good come out of Nazareth?" (John 1:46).

And the answer is a resounding "yes!" Good things come out of small farm towns and fishing villages! As he carried out his ministry, Jesus did so not only in preaching, teaching, and performing miracles; he could often be found at a table with any number of guests. He dined with religious and rebellious alike and never postured himself to gain status in people's eyes, nor did he worry about losing face because some of his company had broccoli in their teeth. More will be said about Jesus's uncanny and unorthodox dining habits in chapter 4, but suffice it to say here that the story of God would first be told around tables, then proclaimed in pulpits, eventually resulting in table celebration again and again.

Church on Mission

Fifty days after Jesus ascended back to the right hand of the Father, he sent the Holy Spirit into the world and into the church to carry on his way of life, bringing God's love, truth, grace, and compassion into every culture around the globe. The gospel would not stay in Jerusalem. It would break the national borders of Israel and find a home in the hearts of millions and millions of people throughout the Roman Empire. Yet we must ask, "What caused the gospel to spread like a grease fire?" Was it a person or personality, a brand or marketing ploy? No. It was a simple meal, telling and retelling the story of God. St. Paul writes, "The Lord Jesus, on the night he was betrayed, took bread, and when he had given thanks, he broke it and said, 'This is my body, which is for you; do this in remembrance of me.' In the same way, after supper he took the cup, saying, 'This cup is the new covenant in my blood; do this, whenever you drink it, in remembrance of me'" (1 Corinthians 11:23-25 NIV).

That evening Paul refers to was Jesus's last celebration of the Passover with the disciples. The ancient story of the Exodus and its message couldn't be any clearer: Jesus was telling the story of God's redemption through a lamb being sacrificed on behalf of the people so that they might be saved. The church, for thousands of years all over the globe, tells this story as often as we gather together in the name of Jesus, the lamb, the centerpiece of the story of God. Each time the church takes communion, that simple meal of bread and wine points forward to another meal—the wedding supper of the Lamb.

Wedding Supper

The story of God concludes with an absolutely glorious wedding banquet! Christ is the groom, the church is the bride, and all creation will resound with the highest praise of God. Sin and death will have been *swallowed up* once and for all; "hallelujahs!" will boom throughout the new heaven and earth. The victory parade will be in full swing. The band will be playing, piñatas will be bursting, and freshly-roasted-coffee-bean joy will fill the air of the dining room of God. The apostle John had a glimpse of this moment and wrote:

> Then I heard what seemed to be the voice of a great multitude, like the roar of many waters and like the sound of mighty peals of thunder, crying out, "Hallelujah! For the Lord our God the Almighty reigns. Let us rejoice and exult and give him the glory, for the marriage of the Lamb has come, and his Bride has made herself ready; it was granted her to clothe herself with fine linen, bright and pure"—for the fine linen is the righteous deeds of the saints. And the angel said to me, "Write this: Blessed are those who are invited to the marriage supper of the Lamb." And he said to me, "These are the true words of God" (Revelation 19:6-9).

As the story of God told in the Bible comes to a close, a sustained note of glory fills our ears and continues forever. There are no snakes, tears, curses, weapons, or tombs in sight. The days of lamentation, starvation, hunger, racism, injustice, violence, and want are in the

past. Shouts of jubilee, praise, exaltation, and otherworldly happiness have filled the bride's heart, and we will finally be perfectly content. The serpent who told Eve to "take and eat" was destroyed by Jesus, who also told his disciples to "take and eat." What went wrong with a meal eaten in sin is healed through the feast and ministry of Christ. Thus, it is only fitting to find Jesus and his bride not at enmity but at the dining table with glasses raised, smiles on their faces, world without end, amen.

QUESTIONS TO CONSIDER

Have you ever thought about God telling his story not just through the pages of Scripture but around the table?

How do you think that can change the way you experience or prepare for your meals?

RECIPES

Breakfast and Brunch

They say that breakfast is the most important meal of the day. These breakfasts and brunches are all so good for different reasons. Or, it's not uncommon for me to take whatever we had the night before and work it into some kind of omelette. For example, last night I made Grilled Chicken Tacos with Spicy Jalapeño Jam, Lime Cabbage, and Black Beans (page 134). The chicken and beans folded perfectly into the omelette with a little cheese and a few flakes of Don Chilio Jalapeño Chili Crisp.

The blueberry smoothie was introduced to me by my friends Gary and Kaylynn Ketterl. The backstory is that I had been battling a never-ending head cold and Gary mentioned that these smoothies had been a game changer for his own immunity. I gave smoothies a go and now I swear by them. The other breakfasts or brunches are quite savory. The Shakshuka is super easy if you happen to make pizzas the night before. Just make extra marinara and you're over halfway done already! The Dungeness Crab Eggs Benedict takes me a little while and is something that I like to break out on a bright summer Saturday here in Seattle. (Especially if one of my friends happened to have taken me crabbing. Then it's a no brainer.)

During the World Cup, one morning our friends Ben and Katie Lacey came over to watch a match. I had been experimenting in the kitchen earlier that morning with seaweed and chili crisp. I made a wrap for Katie and she let out a shout that shook our house much like the hooligans on the tele! The citrusy lime and spicy chili crunch with the rice and eggs will set you up for a victory. Promise.

Blueberry Smoothie

This blueberry smoothie comes to us by way of two people, Gary and Kaylynn Ketterl. The Ketterls are the kind of people every pastor just adores. Consistent encouragers who have a "whatever it takes" mentality when it comes to serving Jesus and his people. One year I had a sinus infection that just would not lift. Gary took note and told me, "I'm not saying this smoothie is the cure, but it just might be!" Not only does this taste amazing but I'm pretty sure it zapped my cold. It's now a regular breakfast around the Early home.

DIRECTIONS

Add all the ingredients to a blender in the order listed and blend to the desired texture, adding more juice or milk if desired.

★ Serves 1 to 2 ★

INGREDIENTS

1½ cups pomegranate juice

½ cup cashew milk

1 cup frozen blueberries

1 cup frozen kale

1 banana

3 T. mixed hemp, chia, and flax seeds

1 T. cinnamon

1 T. turmeric

Shakshuka with Lemon and Feta

This shakshuka is dedicated to the greatest that ever did it-- the illustrator of this very book: Don Clark. One year I was texting with his wife, setting up a time to come over to their home and cook something up to surprise him for his birthday. In a slew of back and forth texting, I failed to indicate that shakshuka was going to be served for breakfast. Erika was naturally assuming nobody would actually show up at 5:00 a.m. to make breakfast...unless that person is yours truly. I arrived at their home, everyone was sound asleep, and I sat in my car for two hours watching the sunrise, reading Colossians, and enjoying the peace and quiet...only to have to leave for my first appointment. I never made Don shakshuka, and so I dedicate this one to him.

DIRECTIONS

Preheat the oven to 375°.

In a large oven-proof skillet or braiser pan over medium heat, add the olive oil and then sauté the onion and bell pepper for a couple of minutes, being careful not to break them down entirely. Then add the garlic and red pepper flakes and cook 1 minute more.

Hand crush the tomatoes into the braiser, then stir in the tomato paste, salt and pepper (at least a teaspoon of each), paprika, and cumin. Allow the mixture to simmer for 15 to 20 minutes, adjusting the heat as needed.

Crack the eggs straight into the sauce, evenly distributing them all around the pan.

Place the pan in the oven and cook for a few minutes to allow the eggs to set nicely.

When the eggs are set to your preference, sprinkle lemon zest, feta cheese, parsley, and shallots evenly over the top of the pan. Serve the shakshuka with thick slices of toast to help sop up the goodness.

★ Serves 4 to 5 ★

INGREDIENTS

3 T. olive oil

1 medium white onion, thinly sliced

1 red bell pepper, thinly sliced

2 T. minced garlic

1 big pinch red pepper flakes (or up to 2 tsp., to taste)

1 (28 oz.) can whole peeled San Marzano tomatoes

1 to 2 T. tomato paste

Salt and pepper, to taste

2 tsp. paprika

2 tsp. ground cumin

6 large eggs

1 lemon, zested

4 T. crumbled feta cheese

2 T. chopped fresh parsley

1 T. pickled shallots

A NOTE ON SALT AND PEPPER: The quality of the salt and pepper you use really does make a difference. I use kosher salt and a pepper grinder for everything in my kitchen. Most recipes just call for "salt and pepper" so use what you like, but for me that always means kosher salt and freshly ground black pepper. A few recipes specifically call for that form of the ingredient when the salt or pepper plays a bigger role in the recipe.

AN APPRECIATION OF BEAUTY AND THE GOOD

Late-night fast food is one of the greatest common graces we enjoy in the world. Here in Seattle, Dick's Drive-In is a staple. This local landmark was established in 1954, and they serve up the absolute best burgers, fries, and shakes, especially after a show or a game. There's never a line; actually, let me rephrase that: there's never a defined line. We Seattleites enjoy standing around like a mob, staring up at the fluorescent lights, all a little angsty, a little passive-aggressive, but also equally charming and endearing. "Oh no! You first! Go ahead." Such is the way of things. And while I would never discourage someone from going to Dick's, we all know that, on a daily basis, we'd definitely be a bit better off dodging the convenience and grease and opting for something a little healthier and that takes a little more time.

Most North Americans I know are *so* busy. We'd do our souls well to intentionally slow down and appreciate the smell of a bushel of strawberries, or savor all that's going on in a gorgonzola salad adorned with the perfect amount of dressing, walnuts, and raisins.

The late Robert Capon encouraged his readers to really become present in the simple things in the kitchen:

Peel an orange. Do it lovingly—in perfect quarters like little boats, or in staggered exfoliations like a flat map of the round world, or in one long spiral, as my grandfather used to do. Nothing is more likely to become garbage than orange rind; but for as long as anyone looks at it in delight, it stands a million triumphant miles from the trash heap.[1]

The writer of Ecclesiastes reminds us that there is "a time for this and a time for that" (Ecclesiastes 3). So yes, there's a time for late-night fast food or the occasional throwback to college dorm ramen. British chef Jamie Oliver is quoted as saying, "The kitchen oven is reliable, but it's made us lazy."

So don't be lazy, don't rush, don't mindlessly tackle tasks, especially when it comes to meal prep. Meals fuel our bodies and bring us together, and preparing a beautiful meal slowly and mindfully provides space and time to engage each of our senses. What do you see? In looking at a perfect rib eye, take time to see the colors, marbling, and textures before you. Everything is as it should be. As the pizza dough nears completion in your mixer, take time to hear the dry flour swish as the dough ball orbits its way around the stainless steel bowl. The next time you make a sausage ragù, don't move so quickly that you forget to deeply inhale the red velvety sauce and rosemary pluming up into the air. As you fillet a salmon, become present. Become conscious not just of the knife in your hand but of the beautiful pink, orange, and white fish lying there on the counter. Place your hand on the scales; slide it down, going with the grain. Oh, and for all that is good and holy in the world, when it's time to eat a taco that you've brought to perfection, don't scarf. Savor it. After all, it is God's gift to you.

Though I can't prove it, I'm pretty sure we all purchase cookbooks by simply looking at the cover and then flipping through the pages—oooing and ahhing over the photos—and then finally splurging so we can add a new favorite to the collection. The recipes here in *Among the Pots and Pans* are all over the map. There's no rhyme or reason to any of them other than they're simply what I love to make for my family and friends. Several of the recipes require some significant time in the kitchen, though there are a few that are quite quick, such as the blueberry smoothie or the traditional shrimp scampi. You'll find what I've already alluded to throughout the book: I'm big on taking my time and being present. Hurrying through the cooking and dining process should be a rarity rather than the norm.

If you choose to cook your way through this book, I'd encourage you to begin by first purging the refrigerator of things you know you'll never use again or that have expired. Do the same with the pantry. Finally, go check out your pots, pans, chef's knives, and cutlery. Sharpen what needs to be sharpened and declutter the place. This is where you're going to spend some time, so you may as well make it a place you'd *want* to be rather than *have* to be. Oh, and if you don't have a good braiser pan, get one! My mother, Bevy, bought me a Le Creuset braiser years ago and it's hands down my favorite thing in my kitchen.

Dungeness Crab Eggs Benedict

DIRECTIONS

Crab Salad

Mix all the ingredients well in a large bowl, cover, and place it in the refrigerator while you prepare everything else.

Hollandaise Sauce

In a small heatproof mixing bowl, whisk together the egg yolks, lemon juice and zest, mustard, and spices. Fill a small saucepan with about 1 inch of water and bring it to a simmer over low heat. Place the mixing bowl atop the saucepan to allow the simmering water to slowly warm the ingredients, whisking constantly and keeping the heat low to avoid curdling the eggs. Slowly whisk in the chopped butter, one or two pieces at a time. Melt and whisk everything together over a period of about 12 to 15 minutes. If necessary, add a little water until the sauce has reached your desired consistency.

Poached Eggs

Bring a medium saucepan of lightly salted water to a gentle simmer. Crack 2 eggs into individual ramekins; don't mix them. Create a small whirlpool in the simmering water with a spoon and carefully slide one of the eggs into the whirlpool. Create another whirlpool and add the other egg. Allow the eggs to swirl and simmer for exactly 3 minutes, adjusting the heat as needed. This is important! Don't boil the eggs! Remove each egg with a slotted spoon to a plate lined with a paper towel and allow the excess water to drain. Repeat the process until all the eggs are done.

Serve

Cut and toast 8 slices of rosemary bread (a salute to Seattle's Lowell's Restaurant!). Onto each slice, spoon crab salad onto the toast as a base layer, then add a poached egg, a scoop of hollandaise sauce, and a sprinkle of chives or tarragon over the top.

★ Serves 4 to 5 ★

INGREDIENTS

Crab Salad

1 lb. Dungeness crab meat

½ lemon, zested and juiced

2 T. minced fresh parsley

2 tsp. salt

1 tsp. pepper

Hollandaise Sauce

4 egg yolks

1 T. lemon juice

2 tsp. lemon zest

1 tsp. Dijon mustard

1½ tsp. salt

1½ tsp. pepper

1 pinch red pepper flakes

16 T. (8 oz.) unsalted butter, chopped into pieces

Water, as needed to thin the sauce

Poached Eggs

8 eggs

Serve

Rosemary bread, from your favorite bakery

Fresh chives or tarragon, chopped

Feta Toast with Jammy Tomatoes and Microgreens

INGREDIENTS

5 Roma tomatoes, quartered

5 cups olive oil

4 whole garlic cloves

5 basil leaves

1 (8 oz.) block feta cheese

1 to 2 cups heavy whipping cream

1 tsp. salt

1 small bunch microgreens

1 grapefruit, zested

1 baguette

6 slices prosciutto (optional)

Salt flakes

DIRECTIONS

Preheat oven to 325°.

Place the tomatoes in a large braiser or other oven-proof pot and add enough olive oil to nearly cover the tomatoes. Add the garlic and basil, then place the braiser in the oven and cook for 1 hour, checking occasionally. The aim is for the tomatoes to break down just a little bit and become "jammy."

While the tomatoes are cooking, prepare the feta and the salad topping.

Crumble the feta into a food processor, then add cream and salt, going easy on the cream—start with one cup, blend on a low speed, and don't add too much too quickly. Watch for the right texture: you essentially want to be able to spread it like warm butter.

Place the microgreens in a small bowl and toss it with the grapefruit zest.

When the tomatoes are done, remove them from the oil and place them in a bowl. Pull them apart using two forks. Drain any excess oil back into the braiser. (You can save the oil for another day.)

Slice the baguette into 6 long diagonal pieces and toast them in the oven for about 4 minutes.

Assembly

Spread a layer of the feta mixture on each piece of toast, top with 1 thin slice of prosciutto, add the warm, jammy tomatoes, then the microgreens. Drizzle with some of the reserved olive oil, and sprinkle with salt flakes.

★ *Makes 6 slices* ★

Seaweed Chili Lime Crunch Wraps

Do you have a friend that when they bite into something glorious all they can do is close their eyes and try not to shout expletives? Well, let me tell you about my friend Katie. Ben and Katie Lacey are two people who have shown us Earlys the love, truth, and generosity of God in countless ways, from boat days on Lake Washington, to wandering endlessly at Disneyland, to tirelessly serving our church, to late night fire pits. These two are as good as it gets. This fun breakfast hit me one morning just as the Lacey family was walking into our home to watch a World Cup game. I'd been fooling around in the kitchen and thought, "Yes, KariKari, seaweed, eggs, lime...all this belongs together." Just as Katie walked in the kitchen and saw what was going on, she took the plate, and said "OH YEAH! LET'S GO!" She took a bite, and it was lights out. No curse words were shouted. Glory came down. I love you, Ben and Katie.

DIRECTIONS

In a small bowl, whisk together the eggs and milk, then pour them into a preheated skillet over medium heat, scrambling them to a light and fluffy texture.

Lay out the seaweed sheets, divide the cooked eggs evenly between them (taco style!) and top with the crunchy chili crisp and a sprinkling of lime zest.

You can also enjoy this wrap with the egg fried instead of scrambled. Try adding a bit of leftover rice for a more substantial meal.

★ Serves 2 ★

INGREDIENTS

2 eggs

2 T. whole milk

4 seaweed sheets

1 T. KariKari garlic chili crisp

1 lime, zested

2

PASSOVER:
The Meal that Saved the Slaves

As the spicy marinara simmers on the stove, our daughter, Tov, takes a warm arancini and baptizes it, submerging the fried rice ball almost completely in the velvety red goodness of the tomato-based sauce. She brings the arancini back to her lips, blows the steam off once, and bites into the cheesy rice ball goodness, one of Italy's greatest gifts to the world. She closes her hazel eyes, savoring the food for all it's worth, and then opens them with an "Mmm . . . Daddy, these are the best we've ever made!" Her name, Tovah, is a Hebrew name that means "God is good." Jana and I love the fact that every single time her name is called throughout her life, her parents, her friends, her enemies, whoever utters it, will be speaking over her "God is good!" What about you? What does your name mean?

And by the way, what's going to be on your kitchen stove this evening? Have you closed your eyes and really savored something as of late?

One of the finest lines in all of the Psalms captures Tov's arancini grin: "Taste and see that the LORD is good. Oh, the joys of those who take refuge in him!" (Psalm 34:8 NLT). King David dined and danced on the heels of the deliverance of God. This is just what we do as we experience firsthand, for ourselves, the grace, kindness, and friendship of the King. Far from being out of the ordinary, David's explosive joy has been the custom of God's children since the very beginning. Four hundred years earlier, Moses's sister Miriam led the Hebrew nation in a song of praise as they found themselves delivered out of slavery and on their way to a land flowing with milk and honey (see Exodus 15).

In the great story of the Exodus, the mighty hand of the Lord was stretched out against the pharaoh and the nation of Egypt. The Egyptians had enslaved the Hebrew people for over four hundred years; interestingly, some of the sprigs that come off the Hebrew word for Egypt mean *cramped*, *restricted*, and *narrow*. God's vision for his people is broad, open, and comfortable, one that gives them plenty of room to live and thrive. The Hebrew people knew this and clung to this truth throughout the incomprehensible turmoil, injustice, and violent suffering; thus the people of God continued to cry out for salvation. God, in his mercy, heard their cries and, in his power, called Moses to lead the people out of bondage. Rather than sending an army, God himself would soon be dressing for battle to go to war on behalf of his chosen people.

Nine devastating plagues befell Egypt, and yet the pharaoh would not relent; he was determined to keep the Hebrews enslaved forever. But he and his army were no match for the Lord Almighty. A tenth plague, the death of the firstborn, swept Egypt, prying the pharaoh's icy death-grip fingers off God's children once and for all.

The tenth plague is quite unique, for not only would it contain a record of the mighty power of God but it would also be the only plague that would accompany a *meal* for those about to be liberated. This meal is known as the Passover; through his creative genius, God used food as a story to forever live on in the theological tastebuds of his children.

My favorite Disney movie is *Ratatouille*. It was the last movie I saw in the theater with my father. Do you recall the food critic, Anton Ego? He was the tall, deathly Dracula figure who growled of his love of food, "If I don't love it, I don't *swallowww*."

When Ego arrived at Gusteau's restaurant in Paris, he was expecting to be grossly disappointed in Chef Linguini's culinary skills. To the food critic's surprise, Remy and Linguini served him the simple peasant dish known as *ratatouille*. The moment Ego took a bite, he was immediately transported in his mind out of Paris, way out into the French countryside, back in time to where he stood in the doorway of his childhood home; there he was a ragged little boy, watching his mother cook. His heart and mind collided as he savored those roasted veggies. What tastes or smells in the kitchen take you back in time?

Scientists tell us that sweets tend to lodge into the hippocampus of our brains, triggering joy and rewards.[1] With this in mind, it makes sense that chocolate seems to get the memories going for me. To this day, if I smell an Oreo cookie, I'm immediately a little boy, playing with Matchbox cars on the fireplace at my MaMa's house. When I taste a rich chocolate mousse, I see my dad standing in the warm yellow sunlight that streams through the window onto his white oxford shirt—knowing full well that soon he'll be wearing a splotch of deep brown sweetness just below his WAE monogram. When I taste hot chocolate, I'm suddenly holding three-year-old Tov's hand as we walk through our neighborhood in Seattle.

Back to the Passover. This first generation of Hebrews had literally, physically, spiritually, and emotionally tasted and seen for *themselves* that the Lord is indeed *good*. And what would be on the menu to forever memorialize God's liberation of his enslaved people? Meat and veggies! As the story goes, God told Moses that the destroying angel would move through Egypt on a particular night and strike down every firstborn in Egypt. However, the Hebrews would be spared so long as they participated in a sacred meal together. First, they were required to sacrifice a lamb and paint the doorframe of their homes in the lamb's blood. Why a blood sacrifice like this? Weren't the Hebrews already God's chosen? Yes, they were. However, they, too, had mingled the worship of God with that of other false gods of Egypt. They were in tremendous need of both physical and spiritual salvation in every sense of the word.

In addition to dining on roasted lamb, they were to eat unleavened bread, and *bitter* herbs. Though the kinds of herbs are not specified, we might assume bitter lettuce was available in that region. (Later on, the Jewish people would associate the bitter herbs with the misery of their ancestors' captivity.) Fittingly, Jesus, who would usher in the greater exodus, was offered *bitter* wine at his crucifixion. God even instructed them about what they were to wear to dinner on that eerie, holy, terrifying, hopeful evening. They were to be dressed, with sandals on and staff in hand, ready to leave at any moment. Moses told them to dine in "haste" or "anxious haste." The reason is that judgment would soon fall, and they were to be prepared to go.

On the evening of destruction, God's people would be identified not by their looks, language, or good works. God was not going to liberate them because of their wealth, education, or morals. Instead, God said, "When I see the blood, I will pass over you" (Exodus 12:13). Through the lamb's sacrifice, the children of God would go free. The lambs were sacrificed on behalf of the people because God *covers* and *cleanses* those he *calls* his own. These people were on their way out of subhuman treatment as machine labor and had their sights set on fully embracing their humanity in the context of the delightful salvation of God.

Humanity at Rest

Human beings are made for more than work, productivity, and creating "content." Genesis tells us that on the seventh day, God rested. God did not need a nap any more than he needs someone to feed him, educate him, or keep him company. God modeled for us the way he wants us to live, which involves disconnecting from work in order that we may rest, play, and provide space to feed not just our bellies but our souls. To intentionally carve out time for this essential rest, doing nothing for ourselves but merely basking in all that God has already provided for us, takes discipline. We in the West specialize in busyness, hurry, and getting more *done*. The anxious turmoil of Egypt makes its way into our world as we buy the lie that somehow if we're not producing something, then we must not be worth anything.

To observe the Sabbath is to take a sledgehammer to the false narratives that plague us day after day after day. It takes courage to walk away and call a day "done." Beyond courage to call it done, Sabbath is our way of embracing that God declares rest to be as natural as work. Sabbath isn't something we earn; it's part of the way things are intended to be under the rule of our Savior. Pastor Eugene Peterson said,

> Sabbath is the time set aside to do nothing so that we can receive everything, to set aside our anxious attempts to make ourselves useful, to set aside our tense restlessness, to set aside our media-satiated boredom. Sabbath is the time to receive silence and let it deepen into gratitude, to receive quiet into which forgotten faces and voices unobtrusively make themselves present, to receive the days of the just completed week and absorb the wonder and miracle still reverberating from each one, to receive our Lord's amazing grace.[2]

The kitchen can become a regular place of Sabbath rest as you chop, dice, slice, and simmer your way through preparing a meal, whether alone or with others. It is a time to see and savor the faithful provision that God has made not only in what simmers on the stove but in reflecting on your own life—your *self*.

QUESTIONS TO CONSIDER

Consider the speed at which you eat, especially with family and friends. Are you hurried or present? After all, the Hebrews dined in haste on *one evening*; but that wasn't the norm.

Soups, Salads, Sides, and More

I spent a lot of time with my grandparents when I was growing up. They were simple, generous people. Each meal always had some kind of side that made their home fragrant and special. Remembering a late summer Monday afternoon at my grandparents' home is how I keep the Sabbath not just in my mind but in my heart—my soul. Here's a daydream of mine:

A soft, warm, yellow light lands on the small wooden desk. Tiny dust particles hang in the sun ray; suspended, moving, living, floating like the universe herself. The guest room bed is perfectly made. The sheets are pulled tight, and the green comforter is tucked neatly beneath the pillows. The smells of toast, detergent, and black tea tiptoe up the stairs and fill the silent room. Within, everything is still. Without, the pine trees sway and a blue jay chirps. I can see my grandfather, Roland, strike a match and light his pipe. He changes the channel. The Braves are winning. A tomato sandwich rests on a paper plate.

In closing my eyes and becoming present, I visit the guest room in me. As I savor the moment, what is simple becomes special.

These soups, salads, and sides become especially wonderful when paired with the weather. The tomato basil soup is perfect for a cold January weeknight when you want something quick but satisfying. The chicken chili is great all through the fall and makes for wonderful leftovers. Arugula mango burrata salad is a great side for anything off the grill through the summer. And the all-wonderful Mexican street corn, a summer staple, belongs on or off the cob and with just about any meal I can think of.

Arancini with Spicy Tomato Dipping Sauce

Arancini have been around forever and there are plenty of different takes on them. I love the ones on Food Network. My friend Jana told me I was missing frozen peas. She was right. Do it!

DIRECTIONS

Pour the broth and salt into a saucepan and bring it to a boil over high heat. Stir in the rice, reduce the heat to low, and simmer, uncovered, until tender, about 20 minutes, adjusting the heat as needed. Spread the rice out on a parchment-lined baking sheet and let it cool completely.

Combine the mozzarella, fontina, pine nuts, and parsley in a bowl; set aside.

Beat the eggs in a large bowl, then stir in the cooled rice, the Parmesan, and ⅔ cup bread crumbs. Shape the mixture into 16 (1½-inch) balls. Put the remaining bread crumbs in a shallow bowl. Punch a hole into the center of each rice ball (I find it easier to use the base of a large chopstick rather than my finger to do this). Into each rice ball, insert 2 teaspoons of the mozzarella mixture and a few peas, then pinch the rice around the filling to enclose. Keep the leftover mixture to top a side salad!

Roll the balls in the bread crumbs and place them on a parchment-lined baking sheet. Loosely cover and refrigerate, at least 1 hour or overnight (if you're going to leave them overnight, they will need more bread crumbs before you fry them the next day).

In a large saucepan over medium heat, pour in ½ inch of vegetable oil and heat until the oil is shimmering. Fry the rice balls, 4 or 5 at a time, turning them regularly until they are golden brown on all sides, about 4 minutes. Remove them with a slotted spoon and drain on paper towels; season them with a little salt while they are still hot. Add more oil if needed to cook the whole batch.

★ **Serves 4 people as an appetizer** ★

Spicy Tomato Dipping Sauce

To make a spicy dipping sauce, simply follow the recipe for Marinara Sauce (page 191), but increase to 2 teaspoons red pepper flakes when you add the tomatoes and tomato paste. Let the sauce simmer for 20 minutes, adding more red pepper as you go to find your desired heat level.

Add the sauce to a blender and blend it to your desired texture. A smoother texture works well for dipping sauces.

INGREDIENTS

3 cups low-sodium chicken broth

¼ tsp. salt

1 cup arborio rice

½ cup shredded mozzarella

½ cup shredded fontina

2 T. pine nuts, toasted

2 T. fresh parsley

2 eggs

½ cup grated Parmesan cheese

1½ cups bread crumbs, divided

½ cup frozen peas

Vegetable oil, for frying

Spicy Tomato Dipping Sauce

Marinara Sauce (page 191)

2 tsp. red pepper flakes

Arugula Mango Burrata Salad

DIRECTIONS

Heat 2 tablespoons olive oil in a skillet on high heat. Cut the cheeks off the mangoes and cube them: Leave the skin on, and put the sharp end of the knife down into the exposed flesh of the mango without going through the skin on the other side. Cut all the way down, making a vertical line. Repeat the process only with horizontal lines, thus making 'cube' shapes. Leave the skin on! Then place the mango cheeks in the oil for 90 seconds to 2 minutes. Let them just begin to turn brown, then remove them from the pan and set them aside to cool. Meanwhile, dice the strawberries and tear up the baby arugula, mint, and parsley in a big bowl. When the browned mangoes have cooled, separate the cubes from the skin by running a knife along the edge of the skin so the cubes fall right off. Add the mango and strawberry pieces to the arugula blend, then tear up one of the burrata balls and add that in as well. Drizzle with the final tablespoon olive oil and a really good balsamic vinegar (we love the OMG! Vanilla Fig Barrel-Aged Balsamic Vinegar), then toss in some salt and pepper, and mix well.

★ Serves 2 ★

INGREDIENTS

1 to 2 mangoes

3 T. olive oil, divided

1 cup sliced or diced strawberries

3 to 4 cups baby arugula

¼ cup fresh mint

¼ cup fresh parsley

1 (4 oz.) burrata cheese ball

Balsamic vinegar, to taste

Salt and pepper, to taste

Mexican Street Corn

INGREDIENTS

4 ears fresh corn, shucked

3 T. olive oil

Salt and pepper, to taste

2 T. mayonnaise

Chili powder

4 T. finely chopped fresh
cilantro

4 limes, juiced

DIRECTIONS

Preheat the oven to 350°.

Place the corn on a baking sheet. Coat the corn with olive oil, add salt and pepper to taste, and roast for about 35 to 40 minutes. Cut the corn off the cobs, and toss it in a bowl with mayo (add more if you like), a sprinkle of chili powder, cilantro, and the lime juice.

★ Serves 4 ★

NOTE: Mexican Street Corn is fantastic on or off the cob! To eat it on the cob, roast it up, then take it out and spread some mayo on the ears. Sprinkle on the other toppings and add some **cotija cheese** or **goat cheese**. It's a perfect side dish for any taco or your favorite grilled meats.

Tomato-Basil Soup

DIRECTIONS

Preheat your oven to 375°. Chop the tomatoes in half, slice the onion into chunks, peel and crush the garlic cloves, then peel the carrots and chop them in half. Place all these vegetables, along with the cherry tomatoes, on a baking sheet. Drizzle the olive oil on top, sprinkle with salt and pepper, then bake in the oven for about an hour. Toss the veggies halfway through.

Remove the baking sheet from the oven and puree its contents in your blender until you get the consistency you like. Blend it longer for a very smooth soup, or a bit less if you like it with more texture.

Pour the contents of the blender into a Dutch oven. Stir in the broth, balsamic vinegar, red pepper flakes, and basil pesto. Cook over medium heat for about 5 minutes, until everything is heated through. To serve, tear apart or chop the mozzarella to use as a topping for the soup, and garnish each bowl with a sprig of basil.

Goes great with a baguette!

★ Serves 4 ★

INGREDIENTS

2 lbs. Roma tomatoes

1 medium onion

7 garlic cloves

3 large carrots

1 lb. cherry tomatoes

⅓ cup olive oil

2 tsp. salt

½ tsp. pepper

4 cups vegetable broth

2 T. balsamic vinegar

½ tsp. red pepper flakes

2 to 3 T. basil pesto

1 ball fresh mozzarella cheese

Fresh basil (garnish)

FIELD TRIPS TO ETHNIC GROCERIES

What are you afraid to cook? Is there a particular cuisine that is completely out of your league? Where do you go out to eat because you just couldn't possibly make that particular dish in your home? For me, it was always any kind of Asian food. There are so many different soy sauces, pastes, spices, and techniques that I assumed would be overwhelming simply because my only knowledge of the food was from when someone else had made it for me. Here in Seattle, though, we live directly behind a glorious Asian market, and I just knew things had to change!

Right inside the market, there's an atrium that houses Rain Café to the left. My friend Kenny, a Japanese brother, owns it. He loves Jesus and always gives me the "family discount." Rain Café is a really fun Japanese restaurant with a big television, a piano, and seating arranged for socializing. It's usually full of high schoolers doing homework, eating shoyu, and drinking bubble tea. Tov and Jana always split a sushi burrito. Within the atrium there's a sauerkraut fish restaurant to the right, a combination travel agency and mobile phone kiosk in the center of the room, and a life-size Goku (for those who don't know, that's a *Dragon Ball Z* anime character).

In the beginning, I would walk around the perimeter of the store, looking at fruits and vegetables I'd literally never seen before in my life. Fruits such as durian, rambutan, and lychee. Vegetables such as gai lan, multiple kinds of choys and cabbages, and water spinach. It was such a fantastic experience! My eyes were opened to an entire world, one I didn't even know existed, and all it cost me was a five-minute walk around the corner. I'll never forget walking down the sidewalk seeing a dozen ducks rotating on the rotisserie next to some bao buns and what looked like pork rinds. I muttered Dorothy's words from the infamous *Wizard of Oz,* "Toto, I have a feeling we're not in Kansas anymore."

Rounding the back of the grocery, I saw all kinds of different noodles, cuts of meat, and live fish to buy from the fishmonger—eels included! For a boy from Woodstock, Georgia, this was all so new and so exciting! At first, I didn't even bother walking the aisles, because I couldn't read anything in there and knew I would just lose hours to curiosity. Eventually I gave in to wandering the aisles, and my desire to learn how to cook Asian cuisine only intensified. One day it struck me: "Wait. Why don't I ask my Japanese, Chinese, and Korean friends to teach me? We hang out all the time anyway!" I pitched the idea of "Field Trip to the Grocery with Alex" to my friends, and they all jumped at the idea.

My friend Mar, Jana's sister, grew up in an Italian-Japanese home. That's right. All the greatest food in the world under one roof. Can you imagine? She and I went to the Asian market, and she

graciously spent time teaching me about all kinds of groceries, candies, and things that would blow this white guy's mind. We came back to my house, turned up Future Islands on the record player, and made her grandmother's dumplings as Mar shared stories about her family, faith, and love of cooking with and for friends.

What about you? Who are your friends? Maybe some field trips are in order!

Mar's Dumplings

DIRECTIONS

Gyoza Filling

Cut out the fibrous center of the cabbage and then wash the leaves thoroughly. Thinly slice the leaves until you have roughly 4 cups. In a colander, sprinkle 4 teaspoons of kosher salt over the sliced cabbage and set it aside while you prepare the rest of the filling.

Place the ground pork in a large bowl and add in the prepared aromatics (green onion, water chestnuts, mushrooms, garlic, and ginger).

In a separate bowl mix together the sesame oil, soy sauce, brown sugar, pepper, and the remaining 1½ teaspoons salt; set aside.

After the salted cabbage has been sitting for 15 to 20 minutes, run it under cold water to rinse several times. Squeeze out the excess water from the cabbage; you should be left with around 2 cups of wilted cabbage.

Add the cabbage to the bowl with the pork and aromatics, then mix until all ingredients seem evenly distributed.

Pour the sesame and soy sauce mixture over the pork mixture and use your hand to combine the ingredients until the mixture becomes sticky.

> **TIP:** Sauté 1 tablespoon of the filling in a frying pan and taste it to make sure it is seasoned to your liking.

Wrappers

In a mixing bowl, combine the flour and salt. Slowly mix in the water in 3 parts, using your fingers to incorporate the flour and water into a shaggy dough ball.

Knead the dough for 7 to 10 minutes until the dough has changed texture and become smooth.

Roll the dough into a log and let it rest for 30 minutes to an hour. This is an important step, as it allows the gluten to relax and will give your dough better extensibility when rolling it out.

Take the dough log and chop it into about 50 pieces. Roll each piece into a ball that is around 3 centimeters in diameter, a little larger than a grape.

One at a time, flatten each dough ball on your countertop with the heel of your palm to create a pancake shape. Using a rolling pin, roll the dough into a thin disc, rotating 90 degrees with every pass until you get a circle that is about 3 inches in diameter. Dust the finished wrappers with potato starch to prevent sticking.

INGREDIENTS

Gyoza Filling

1 head napa cabbage

5½ tsp. kosher salt, divided

1 lb. ground pork (preferably Kurobuta)

½ cup chopped green onion

¼ cup water chestnuts, drained and roughly diced

2 T. chopped shiitake mushrooms

2 large garlic cloves, minced

1 T. fresh grated ginger

2 T. toasted sesame oil

2 tsp. soy sauce

2 tsp. brown sugar

Pinch ground black pepper

Wrappers

You can either buy round, pre-made wrappers at any Asian market or use the recipe below.

300 grams flour

½ tsp. salt

150 ml. boiling water

Potato starch for dusting

Cooking Slurry (Optional):

⅓ cup water

3 tsp. flour

1½ T. neutral cooking oil

Dash of salt

Oil, for frying

Dipping Sauce:

2 T. unseasoned rice vinegar

2 T. soy sauce

2 tsp. of your favorite chili crisp (optional)

TIP: Rolling the dough and folding the pleats can be difficult to get right and are better learned with detailed visuals. I recommend watching videos of the correct method to improve your practice!

Assembly and Cooking

Use water to slightly moisten the edges of a wrapper and then place a small amount of filling in the center. Fold the dough in half over the filling so that it looks like a semicircle, then use your thumb and index finger to pinch 5 to 6 pleats across the top of the gyoza to seal in the filling.

If you want to create a fried lace skirt around your dumplings, then whisk together the ingredients for the slurry and set aside. If not, then skip to the next step.

When you are ready to cook the gyoza, heat a tablespoon of neutral oil (such as canola oil) in a non-stick skillet over medium heat. When the oil is hot enough, place the gyoza in the pan, a few at a time so as not the crowd the pan, and fry for a few minutes until the bottom starts to look golden.

Pour the prepared slurry into the pan—if you are not doing this step then pour 2 to 3 tablespoons of plain water into the pan. Quickly cover it with a lid. Let the gyoza steam on medium-low heat to ensure the filling is cooked through. After 4 to 6 minutes, remove the lid and let the excess water cook off. Once the gyoza bottoms become crispy, use tongs to remove them to a paper towel–lined plate and keep warm.

Continue cooking batches of gyoza. Be sure to do the whole process of heating oil, cooking, steaming, and crisping each batch. When you remove the last batch, turn off the heat and serve the gyoza with the dipping sauce.

★ Makes about 50 pieces ★

White Chicken Chili

Serve this with Pickled Onion, Toasted Cumin Sour Cream
(page 145), and a side of Bacon-Encrusted Cornbread (page
64). There ya have it! Add some avocado slices and cilantro too!

DIRECTIONS

Preheat your grill to 400°, and preheat your broiler.

Cut slits across the chicken breasts that are about 1 inch apart (see Tips for Grilling Chicken, page 121). Salt and pepper the chicken liberally, using about 1 teaspoon of each, then drizzle with 1 tablespoon olive oil and place the chicken on the hot grill. Cook it for about 10 minutes, flipping once halfway through.

Meanwhile, shuck the corn, drizzle it with olive oil, sprinkle with salt and pepper to taste, and place it on a baking pan. Broil it about 15 minutes or until roasted to your preference, shaking the pan every 4 or 5 minutes to get an even roast.

While the chicken and corn are cooking, heat 2 tablespoons of olive oil in a large pot or Dutch oven over medium heat. Add the onion and about ½ teaspoon each salt and pepper (or to taste) and cook the onion to soften.

Pull the chicken from the grill once it's fully cooked, then cut it into bite-size pieces. Add the chicken to the pot, then add the cumin, coriander, all 3 cans of beans, the tomatoes, and about 9 ounces of the beer. When the corn is done, cut the corn kernels off the cobs and add the kernals to the pot as well. Turn it down to simmer, and cook for 15 minutes, stirring so as to ensure nothing sticks to the bottom.

Combine the remaining beer and the masa harina in a bowl. Mix it well with a fork and add it to the chili. Keep an eye on the heat and let the chili simmer slowly, stirring it occasionally and adjusting the heat as necessary. Simmer for another 25 minutes as you turn your attention to the cornbread and toppings. Taste the chili every so often and add more salt and pepper if needed.

To serve, ladle the chili into bowls, add a bit of pickled onion, a dollop of sour cream, some sliced avocado, and a few cilantro leaves. And trust me, you don't want to miss out on the Bacon-Encrusted Cornbread!

★ Serves 4 ★

INGREDIENTS

2 boneless, skinless chicken breasts (about 1 lb.)

2 tsp. salt, divided

2 tsp. pepper, divided

3 to 4 T. olive oil, divided

1 yellow onion, diced

3 ears corn

1 tsp. ground cumin

1 tsp. ground coriander

1 (15 oz.) can kidney beans

1 (15 oz.) can black beans

1 (15 oz.) can pinto beans

1 (15 oz.) can fire-roasted tomatoes

1 (12 oz.) beer (I use Corona)

⅓ cup masa harina (this is the best—Mexican flour in chili!)

Toppings

Avocado

Cilantro

Pickled Onion (page 145)

Toasted Cumin Sour Cream (page 145)

Bacon-Encrusted Cornbread

INGREDIENTS

7 strips bacon

1 cup cornmeal

½ cup all-purpose flour

1 tsp. salt

¼ cup shortening

1 cup milk

1 egg

1 tsp. baking soda

DIRECTIONS

Preheat the oven to 450°.

Fry the bacon in a skillet and chop it to desired size.

Mix the cornmeal, flour, and salt in a bowl and set it aside.

Melt the shortening in a saucepan.

Mix the milk, egg, and baking soda in a measuring cup, whisking it with a fork until it is well blended.

Pour the milk mixture and the melted shortening into the cornmeal mix, then stir well.

Grease a 10-inch oven-safe skillet, sprinkle the bacon pieces over the bottom, then pour in the cornmeal batter.

Bake for about 15 to 20 minutes or until golden brown.

★ Serves 4 to 8 ★

Tov's Panna Cotta

Palm Springs, California is a place where many of us Seattle-ites choose to get away for Spring Break. After enduring the long grey months of November through February, Palm Springs truly is like an oasis. One evening, while the kids were swimming in the pool, I went out to pick up some Italian food and bring it back. Of course, we can't skip out on dessert, so naturally I bought a panna cotta for our daughter, Tov. In fact, I bought two, knowing that she would absolutely love it! She ended the day wrapped in a towel, sitting by a fire pit outside, eating a panna cotta, with some Sinatra quietly playing. The next morning, I brought the second panna cotta to her for breakfast in bed. She was in heaven and so was I. Of all the panna cottas we've made over the years, Epicurious's is hands down the best we've ever had. This is adapted from their recipe, with Tov's favorite toppings of Fran's raspberry sauce and mint leaves.

DIRECTIONS

This one is easy for those like Tov who both want to spend time in the kitchen but also reserve the right to bolt off and go be a teenager. Add the cold water to a small saucepan and then sprinkle the gelatin over the water. Let it stand about 1 minute; it will begin to take on a new shape, looking a bit like the surface of Mars with all the ripples and rivets. Then turn on the heat to low and stir until all the gelatin is dissolved. While I'm doing this, Tov will get a larger saucepan and bring the cream, half and half, and sugar just to a boil, stirring constantly. From there she will remove the pan from the heat and stir in the gelatin mixture and vanilla. I then divide the cream mixture among ramekins (use eight ½-cup or four 1-cup ramekins) and allow it to cool to room temperature.

Drizzle Fran's raspberry sauce over the panna cotta and top it with fresh mint leaves.

★ Serves 4 to 8 ★

INGREDIENTS

1 envelope unflavored gelatin (about 1 T.)

2 T. cold water

2 cups heavy cream

1 cup half and half

⅓ cup sugar

1½ tsp. vanilla extract

1 T. Fran's raspberry sauce

1 small bunch mint leaves

Caramel Custard Bread Pudding

INGREDIENTS

1 (18 oz.) loaf brioche bread

3¾ cups whole milk

1½ cups heavy cream

1¼ cups sugar

1¼ tsp. vanilla

¾ tsp. cinnamon

7 large eggs

Bourbon Sea Salt Caramel (page 69)

Serve

Vanilla ice cream

DIRECTIONS

Begin this dish the night before you plan to enjoy it.

Cut the bread into 1 to 1½-inch cubes. I use three-day-old bread and I lightly toast the cubed bread in the oven.

Prepare the custard: In a mixing bowl, whisk together the milk, cream, sugar, vanilla, and cinnamon. In a separate bowl, whisk the eggs until they are fully combined, not showing any separation of the whites and yolks, then add the eggs into the milk mixture.

Place the toasted bread into a 9 × 13-inch glass baking dish. Pour the custard over the cubes and gently stir together until all the bread is coated.

Cover the dish and leave it in the refrigerator overnight until all the mixture has been soaked up.

When you are ready to bake, preheat your oven to 350°.

Cover your baking dish tightly with foil and place it into a large roasting pan. This is important! Fill the large roasting pan with water to make a water bath that comes halfway up the outside of the baking dish containing your bread pudding.

Bake the pudding for 1½ to 2 hours covered, or until the custard is set and a fork inserted in the middle comes out clean. Leaving the baking dish in the water bath, remove the foil and continue to bake, uncovered, until the crust turns a little brown. Meanwhile, prepare the caramel.

Serve

Drizzle a little caramel on a plate.
Put down a square portion of pudding. (Warm is best!)
Top it with more caramel.
Add a dollop of vanilla ice cream.
Drizzle caramel on top.

★ Serves 8 ★

Bourbon Sea Salt Caramel

Set out the cream and butter to come to room temperature. If your cream is still cold when you need to add it to the recipe, you can microwave it for about 15 seconds to get it to room temperature. The butter also must be at room temperature; I thinly slice the butter to warm it up faster. Set these aside as you prepare the caramel.

Whisk together the sugar and water in a small saucepan. Turn the burner to medium and do not touch the sugar mixture as it heats up. Bring it to a simmer and leave it alone until it starts to change color.

When it turns a copper color, immediately remove the pan from the burner and slowly add the heavy cream. Stir until combined, then stir in the room-temperature butter. Finally, add the bourbon, vanilla, and sea salt. Stir to combine.

Use it immediately or store it in the refrigerator. This is a constant ingredient at my house!

Bourbon Sea Salt Caramel

½ cup heavy whipping cream, room temperature

¼ cup butter, room temperature

1 cup white sugar

¼ cup water

2 T. bourbon

1 tsp. vanilla extract

1 tsp. fine sea salt

3

JESUS FEEDS FIVE THOUSAND:
The Kitchen of Compassion

"For many were coming and going, and they had no leisure even to eat" (Mark 6:31). Though it's not in any of our early Greek manuscripts, I kind of wonder if there just may be a lost Gospel of Mark out there somewhere that says, *"And they were hangry!"* *Hanger* is what happens when our growling stomachs turn us into growling people. Prior to 2018, the word *hangry* wasn't found in the *Oxford English Dictionary*. However, we all knew what it meant long, long before it passed for entry into the dictionary. *Hanger* is what happens when our attitudes are taken hostage by our appetites.

Hanger can truly bring out the worst in us; it can turn a perfectly pleasant day into a full-blown nightmare. Think back to the last time you were at the "happiest place on earth," Disneyland. Do you remember the child in line that had an absolute meltdown because he was "starving to death"? Was it your child? Was it *you*? We parents know that pain all too well, and it usually only takes one ear-piercing shrill of misery to teach us the lesson: always, always, *always* have a snack. If you're planning on having kids at any point in your life, take it from us sage parents who have gone before you and suffered to bring you this pearl of great price: always have a snack! You can forget almost anything—keys, wallet, phone, your social security number, whatever—but if you don't have a granola bar, applesauce pouch, goldfish crackers, or some fruit slices, you'll be doomed to suffer the wrath of a child. Our bellies can turn angels into demons so quickly, can't they?

Yet our gastrointestinal system doesn't just report negative emotions; our stomachs can also serve as the birthplace of the feelings that make life worth *living*. It's down in our bellies where the deepest movements of love, grace, and compassion originate. In fact, Jesus's most famous miracle, which happens to involve food, gives us a glimpse into the compassionate heart of God through the *stomach* of our Savior.

The Compassionate Nature of the Kingdom

The feeding of the five thousand is the *only* miracle recorded in all four Gospels.[1] We can only speculate as to why the Evangelists were more committed to reporting this miracle than any other; perhaps no miracle better captures the *compassionate* nature of the kingdom and kitchen of God. Mark's Gospel tells us that Jesus had sent the disciples to drive out demons (Mark 6:7). When they returned, they "told him all that they had done and taught" (verse 30). Okay, so far, so good. But then Mark includes a verse that means as much to me as the infamous words of John 3:16. We learn that the disciples were so busy with the ministry "that they did not even have a chance to eat" (verse 31 NIV). As a pastor, I can assure you that adding hanger pains to ministry is a perfect recipe for exhaustion, irritation, and moodiness.

Every Sunday morning, I get up very early to pray, read my sermon manuscript, and prepare to head to the church building. I'll gather with our staff and volunteers, connect with the saints, meet new people, and then finally preach the gospel at some point during our liturgy. After the sermon, our congregation takes communion, sings to the King, and then I will get up and raise my hands for the bene-diction; the people open their hands in a receiving posture and the blessing of God is spoken with the concluding words "Go in peace." It's at that time that our church lovingly turns to friends and begins talking and catching up, which goes on for quite some time until we have to kick people out. When I finish praying with people and setting up times to connect throughout the week, I'll climb into my nearly twenty-year-old toaster-box Honda Element, and head home. There can often be any number of feelings circulating—fatigue, excitement, sadness, concern, curiosity, you name it. And if I'm going to act like the Christ that I just proclaimed to the congregation, I'd certainly better eat something; otherwise my poor family will have to endure a grumpiness of incalculable proportions. A glorious beef roast is the perfect meal designed to satisfy the soul and stomach as a Sunday afternoon nap looms on the horizon.

Jesus had suggested that the disciples get away "to a desolate place and rest a while" (Mark 6:31). As they made their way across the lake, an enormous crowd of primarily Jewish people spotted them, then "ran there on foot" and "got there ahead of them" (verse 33). Certainly the weary and hungry disciples were less than excited about another crowd in need. It's one thing to plan a dinner party and have all your ducks in a row; it's another thing to dig deep and serve others spontaneously when all you really want is to just sit on the couch in your sweatpants, eat gelato, and fall asleep watching a movie.

However, Mark records that when *Jesus* saw the crowd, "he had *compassion* on them, because they were like sheep without a shepherd" (6:34, emphasis added). The tender concern of Jesus arose not from his mind nor from his heart but from his *stomach*. The Greek word for *compassion* (*splachnizomai*, pronounced "splahgh-kneetz-oh-my) comes from the word *splachna*, which means "stomach, guts, bowels, or entrails." Why is this important? Because in the ancient world, people understood that the most intense emotions arose from deep down within the hidden self, from the gut, the *splachna*.

Essentially, the Gospel teaches us that Jesus's *gut was wrenched*. He saw more than hungry mouths to feed; he saw image bearers who needed the truth of God explained to them clearly and shown tangibly.

Integrated Theology: Heart and Hands

Mark notes the crowds were "like sheep without a shepherd." Using the metaphor of shepherding was an ancient way in which the people of Israel thought of those tasked with priests. The sixth-century BC prophet Ezekiel rebuked the wicked priests of his day because they were guilty of neglecting, abusing, and taking advantage of the people they were supposed to be teaching, caring for, and protecting. As a result, God promised he would come down and shepherd the people *himself* (Ezekiel 34:11-12). Ezekiel's warning went unheeded; Jesus arrived on the scene only to find the *same* kind of leaders still getting away with the same kinds of evil.

Thus, he condemned the hypocritical leaders, who "preach, but do not practice" (Matthew 23:3); who "tie up heavy burdens, hard to bear, and lay them on people's shoulders, but they themselves are not willing to move them with their finger" (verse 4); who "shut the kingdom of heaven in people's faces" (verse 13). In this sobering moment of accountability, Jesus left no stone unturned, even down to the kitchen spice rack and dinnerware. "You tithe mint and dill and cumin, and have neglected the weightier matters of the law: justice and mercy and faithfulness" (verse 23). Yes! Even their *spice racks* weren't safe from his perfect assessment of their phony, burdensome, joyless spirituality! He went on to show them the way of God: "First clean the inside of the cup and the plate, that the outside also may be clean" (verse 26). When Jesus sees his people wandering aimlessly without leadership or suffering under poor leadership, he speaks truth to those in power and extends grace to those who are hungry, hurting, and rootless. These passages serve both to warn and to comfort us. To those in any form of leadership, serve diligently with integrity, grace, and presence; to those who have been wounded by poor leaders, God is on your side.

When the New Testament uses the word *compassion*, it does not mean to merely have momentary feelings of pity on others. *Compassion* always has words, hands, and feet attached to it. Thus, Jesus fed the people's souls *and* their stomachs. Mark 6:34-44 tells it this way: Moved, by compassion, "he began to teach them many things." As the teaching continued, the hungry disciples approached Jesus and suggested that he send the crowd away to "buy themselves something to eat."

Do you think they were concerned about everyone else getting a meal? Maybe. My gut tells me that if they were anything like me, they were guilty of attempting to hurry Jesus up so they might get the rest and meal their own bodies were craving. Jesus quipped, "You give them something to eat." Perhaps shocked, frustrated, and embarrassed, they asked whether they should empty their bank account to feed the masses. Jesus told them to go and see what food they could find. John 6:9 tells us that a little boy gave his lunch to the disciples, and the disciples gave it to Jesus. Having the little lunch in his hands, Jesus then had everyone sit down in groups of fifty or a hundred on the green grass. Sidenote: Throwing a dinner party for a few friends can be pretty challenging; imagine organizing all these people to sit down in groups the way Jesus asked! After everyone had sat down, Jesus looked up to heaven, said a blessing, broke the fish and loaves, and gave the food to the disciples to give to everyone to eat.

Hospitality and Trust

Pause: Have you ever gone to the grocery store hungry? Or worse, cooked while hungry? Argh! The famished disciples were tasked with handing out food to the masses. And the food continued to multiply until all the people ate and were satisfied! Can you imagine the kinds of questions the disciples must've been getting as they brought the food to the people? "Who is that down there? Where are you getting all the food? Are we going to run out?" Yet the food supply did not run out. At the end of the day, Jesus instructed the disciples to collect all the broken pieces. The leftovers totaled twelve baskets. One basket for each disciple.

That's the story of Jesus's most famous miracle, and it corresponds to David's most famous psalm. In Psalm 23 (emphasis added), David writes, "The Lord is my *shepherd*; I shall not want. He makes me lie down in *green* pastures. . . You prepare a table before me in the presence of my enemies. . . My cup overflows."

David envisioned the Lord as the great *shepherd* who gave his *sheep* rest upon the *green grass* as he happily prepared a dining *table* for them even as they were surrounded by enemies. Such beauty, provision, and kindly peacefulness describe Almighty God's consistent, compassionate heart and hands.

Within a few days of feeding the five thousand kosher Jews, Jesus found himself in a place inhabited primarily by *Gentile* people. To the Jews, Gentiles were considered unclean outsiders belonging not to God but to the ways of the world. They ate pork and shellfish. They didn't carry on the traditions of the Jews, and they most certainly didn't abide by the law of Moses. Yet they were no bother to Jesus, and when he was in town, they, too, found him irresistible. A crowd numbering upwards of four thousand people had been lingering around Jesus for three days. Jesus could see the hunger on their faces, and he said to his disciples, "I have *compassion* on the crowd, because they have been with me now three days and have nothing to eat. And if I send them away hungry to their homes, they will faint on the way. And some of them have come from far away" (Mark 8:3, emphasis added).

Jesus's compassion was not limited to only fellow Jewish people. His kitchen was open to everyone. His loving posture extended to all kinds of people because *every* human being is made in the image and likeness of God. God's compassion cannot be bound by anything! Ethnicity, skin color, politics, belief system, or anything else that tears people apart is no match for God's heart for his image bearers. As we grow in the grace of God, we, too, begin to experience his compassion flowing through us, and in time we begin to change. Before long, we strive for selflessness over the competition, servanthood over egoism, and generosity over stinginess. Beloved Brennan Manning reminds us, "Our culture says that ruthless competition is the key to success. Jesus says that ruthless compassion is the purpose of our journey."[2] No teaching, parable, or sermon was recorded at the feeding of the four thousand. On this day, the disciples searched and brought Jesus seven loaves of bread and a "few small fish." Again, Jesus blessed the food, multiplied it, and fed the masses until they were "satisfied." Over nine thousand people encountered Jesus at these two gatherings, and he did more than speak the words of life; he gave them bread and fish, carbohydrates and protein, and they ate until they were *satisfied*.

QUESTIONS TO CONSIDER

Have you ever experienced God's compassion for *you*?
Not just the world, the church, or the crowds
but you personally? If so, what was that like,
and how did it impact you?

After reading of Jesus's gut-wrenching compassion
for the crowds that led him to teach and serve,
how might you go and do the same?

Seafood

Here in Seattle, we *love* our salmon. I've been graced to have friends who take me out fishing for coho and king salmon every year. The early mornings before work really are beyond words. Puget Sound is still, the sun is rising, the colors are changing, the mountains are peeking out in every direction, and the seagulls are mewing. All is beautiful, peaceful, and idyllic until suddenly the sea lions break out into barking at one another, fighting for the best position to lie in the sun on a buoy.

Here in the seafood chapter, I share a salmon and salad that was inspired by a chef at a winery that Jana and I have been members of for years here in Seattle. The other seafoods here are some that I've grown to love sharing with family and friends. One is the swordfish! This is a fish that comes from the coast of California and Hawaii. The texture is similar to that of a pork chop. It is versatile and supertasty! This is even a fish for those who avoid fish. It can be served in any number of ways. My favorites are either grilled with veggies or as a sandwich.

The cod ceviche with mango is perfect for a hot summer day or evening as you wind down from an afternoon of swimming. It's cool, light, and not too filling. The traditional shrimp scampi is a quick and easy recipe for a weeknight with family, or if you are cooking for one, this makes a simple leftover for lunch the following day.

Grilled Salmon Toast with Pickled Onion, Dill Mayo, and Capers

DIRECTIONS

Prepare the salmon by patting it dry with a paper towel and allowing it to come up to room temperature. Then sprinkle it with salt and pepper and add a good drizzle of olive oil. Don't oil the grill, just the fish. Set the fish aside while you prepare the pickled onion and mayo.

In a bowl, toss together the red onion, vinegar, lime, and sugar, then place the bowl in the refrigerator.

In another small bowl, stir all the mayo ingredients together, then cover the bowl and place it in the refrigerator.

Now it's time to grill the salmon. Heat a charcoal grill to around 450° and then place the salmon directly over the coals, skin down. Don't flip the salmon. Keep an eye on it and turn it a quarter turn about every 3 minutes until it looks done. You will notice that the salmon will begin to change color at the bottom, from dark to a more pale color, as the heat works through the salmon skin to the fish itself. Top the salmon with lemon slices (feel free to slice and use the one you zested), and let it rest while you toast the bread. Sometimes I'll drizzle it with honey just before serving.

Cut the loaf of ciabatta bread into about 10 slices and toast them lightly on the grill or under the broiler. Spread each slice with mayo, flake the salmon on top, then add capers and onion to taste.

★ Serves 6 ★

INGREDIENTS

Salmon

1½ lbs. coho salmon fillet, skin on

Salt and pepper, to taste

1 to 2 T. canola oil

Pickled Onion

1 red onion, thinly sliced

½ cup apple cider vinegar

2 limes, juiced

1 T. sugar

Mayo

1 cup mayonnaise

1 lemon, zested

½ lemon, juiced

1 tsp. dried dill weed

½ tsp. garlic powder

Serve

2 lemons, sliced

Ciabatta bread

Honey (optional)

Capers, jarred (to finish)

SEAFOOD

> **GRILLING:** I personally like to grill over charcoal on a Weber. I love it. I know Big Green Egg and Traegers are awesome, but I just prefer to work with things a bit more as I cook. If you have a different kind of grill, you may need to adjust the heat or cooking time based on what works best with your grill.

Smoked Salmon
with Cilantro Sauce

For a spectacular meal, serve this with the Arugula Mango Burrata Salad on page 51.

DIRECTIONS

For the sauce, simply blend all the ingredients in a food processor until the sauce is smooth. Check the consistency and taste, and increase the processing time or quantity of ingredients as necessary for desired texture and flavor. Set aside and leave at room temperature.

Place the wood chips into a large bowl. Cover with about 2 cups of water and allow the chips to soak for 30 minutes. Then move on to the salmon.

For the salmon, get your charcoal grill going, grouping the coals in one half of the grill. Place a pan of water on the grill grate, on the opposite side from the coals. Put the cooking grate back in place, cover the grill, and let it heat up to about 220°.

Blend the spices together in a small bowl, then sprinkle the seasoning mix liberally on both sides of the salmon, and drizzle it with olive oil. Place the salmon on the grill skin side down, directly over the pan of water. Drain the woodchips and then add them directly to the coals. Replace the lid on the grill, and cook the salmon for about 2 hours on indirect heat.

Plate the salmon, drizzle it with the cilantro sauce, and serve it with the Arugula Mango Burrata Salad. Perhaps some rosé would pair well.

★ Serves 4 ★

INGREDIENTS

Cilantro Sauce

1 cup fresh cilantro leaves

½ cup chopped fresh chives

1 to 2 garlic cloves

¼ cup olive oil

1 T. lime juice

1 T. white or apple cider vinegar

Salt and pepper, to taste

2 cups hickory wood chips

Salmon

1½ lbs. salmon fillet, skin on

2 tsp. ground cumin

1 tsp. smoked paprika

1 tsp. ground coriander

1 tsp. rosemary flakes

¾ tsp. salt

¼ tsp. pepper

Olive oil

Grilled Swordfish

INGREDIENTS

4 (6 oz.) 1-inch-thick swordfish steaks

3 T. olive oil

4 tsp. low-sodium soy sauce

1 T. red wine vinegar

1 T. honey

1 T. grated fresh ginger

2 T. minced garlic

Pinch red pepper flakes

3 rosemary sprigs

½ lemon, zested

DIRECTIONS

In a bowl, whisk together everything except the swordfish. Pat the swordfish steaks dry with a paper towel, then put them into a gallon-size resealable plastic bag and pour the marinade over the steaks. Allow the steaks to marinate at room temperature for about 15 minutes.

Preheat your grill to 425°. Discard the marinade and grill the swordfish, staying mindful that it is a slightly tougher fish (think: pork chops) and most desire it to be well done. I grill swordfish for about 5 minutes per side, flipping once.

Once the fish is cooked, serve it with your desired side, or you could also turn this into a great sandwich by taking the grilled swordfish, cutting it to appropriate sizes, and serving it on focaccia bread with a slice of tomato and some tahini sauce, garnished with fresh mint.

★ *Serves 4* ★

SERVING THE MARGINS

As Christians, we often equate biblical hospitality with daily life in a community with Jesus at the center. What I mean is this: life in regular community often involves having meals in one another's homes, praying together, reading the Bible, and enjoying each other's company. But *biblical hospitality*, especially according to Jesus, is far more sacrificial. Some of Jesus's most jarring words around his version of hospitality are shocking for many Western believers. For instance, he said, "But when you give a feast, invite the poor, the crippled, the lame, the blind" (Luke 14:13). That's radical hospitality!

Jesus teaches his followers to budget time, money, and meals for those who would've otherwise been pushed to the margins of society. Such a teaching would have shocked his hearers as much as it shocks us today. Recall that in his context, many religious people believed that if someone was physically suffering, such would have been due to the fact that the individual had somehow offended God. Remember Job's friends? Essentially, they asked Job, "What did you do to upset God so much that he punished you this severely?" Or consider the question posed to Jesus in John's Gospel: "Why was this man born blind? Who sinned, him or his parents?" Yet Jesus didn't support that kind of karma-theology. He taught that rain falls "on the just and the unjust" (Matthew 5:45). Rather than walking around with a clipboard, making sure everyone "gets what they deserve," he lived and called us to embody compassion.

Think about our context in North America, in the United States and other Western countries. Who are the marginalized? The poor, the stranger, and the lonely immediately come to mind. Think of Title I schools, unhoused neighbors, refugees, and elderly in your community. These are the people who are often pushed into cramped spaces, who often carry about feelings of fear and worthlessness. How might you and your church begin to move toward those who society overlooks? Here at our church in Seattle, we partner with other nonprofits that care for our unhoused neighbors. We're able to come into the facility, cook meals with and for people, and we run several clothing drives throughout the year. For Title I schools, we stay closely connected to the teachers and intentionally reach out to see what kind of needs we can tangibly meet, given that these schools are often underfunded. For the elderly, we have a reading and discussion group, and we bring in a Christmas choir to sing one evening during Advent. When it comes to refugees, we partner with other local nonprofits or churches that are primarily comprised of members of an ethnic group that have fled to Seattle for asylum. We have been able to open our homes to help our brothers and sisters as they get on their feet, as well as donate food and clothing to people of all ages. Those who are pushed out into the margins occupy the very center of the heart of God. Remember, "the last will be first, and the first will be last" (Matthew 20:16 NIV).

Crab Cakes with Rémoulade and Duck-Fat Fries

This recipe gives you a lot of room to wing it and customize, without worrying about precise measurements. The amounts listed are about what I normally do, but you can easily make a bigger batch of fries, a spicier crab cake, or a different salad. Feel free to make the rémoulade and salad dressing ahead of time and pull them out when needed.

DIRECTIONS

Fries go first: Take a thin slice off the top and bottom of each potato, and then quarter the potatoes lengthwise to make supreme fries. Take your supreme fries and soak them in cold water for at least 30 to 60 minutes.

Then dry them on a cookie sheet layered with a paper towel.

Preheat the oven to 400°. Discard the paper towel, and coat your cut fries with olive oil and a little salt and pepper. Roast them for 20 minutes, then flip or shuffle the fries and roast for another 15 minutes. Remove from the oven and allow them to cool. Turn off the oven.

In a wok or Dutch oven, heat a neutral oil and the duck fat to 375° to 400°. Fry the supreme fries in batches for 5 to 6 minutes until they are crispy and golden brown. Drain them on a new cookie sheet lined with paper towels as you cook the remaining batches. Place all the drained fries into the warm (but turned off!) oven to let them stay warm.

While fries are soaking or roasting, prepare the crab cakes: Use a food processor to turn the golden crackers into bread crumbs. Add them to a large bowl, along with the crab and all remaining ingredients for the crab cakes except for the flour. I am not very specific on my sour cream and Worcestershire measurements, and you can adjust the type and amount of peppers to your own taste. Mix it gently with a plastic spatula to form a dough-like texture. Line a cookie sheet with wax paper or parchment paper. Wet your hands

INGREDIENTS

Fries

5 medium round russet potatoes

Salt and pepper, to taste

Extra-virgin olive oil

32 oz. neutral frying oil (such as sunflower, safflower, canola or grape-seed oil)

⅓ cup duck fat

Cajun spice or Old Bay Seasoning, to taste

Crab Cakes

1 to 2 sleeves golden crackers, such as Ritz (about 5 to 6 oz.)

24 oz. crab meat

2 egg yolks

¼ cup sour cream, or more to taste

¼ cup Worcestershire sauce

1 lemon, zested and juiced

1 bunch chives, thinly sliced

2 T. Dijon or stone-ground mustard

1 large jalapeño or serrano pepper, diced

All-purpose flour, for dredging

Rémoulade

½ cup mayo or sour cream (or a mixture of the two)

2 T. Dijon or stone ground mustard

1 tsp. Cajun seasoning

1 T. smoked paprika

1 T. honey

Salt and pepper, to taste

1 T. capers, or more to taste

3 cloves garlic, minced

½ lemon, juiced

Fresh parsley and dill, chopped, to taste

Salad

1 large English cucumber, sliced

4 small to medium-size heirloom tomatoes, sliced

1 small red onion or shallot, sliced

2 to 4 oz. feta cheese, crumbled

Dijon Salad Dressing

½ lemon, juiced

1 T. Dijon mustard

2 T. champagne vinegar

4 T. good extra-virgin olive oil

Salt and pepper, to taste

Fresh oregano, chopped, to taste

and roll the crab mixture into palm-size balls—bigger than a golf ball but smaller than a baseball. Dredge the balls lightly with all-purpose flour. Be sure not to let the flour clump!

Place the crab cakes on the prepared cookie sheet and put them in the fridge for at least 30 minutes to chill and firm.

After the cakes have chilled and you are done frying the potatoes, fry the crab cakes in the same oil for 2 to 3 minutes on each side, till golden. Don't overcook.

Serve the crab cakes and the supreme fries with the rémoulade. The fresh flavors of the salad make a perfect accompaniment to this meal!

★ Serves 4 ★

Rémoulade

Mix together all ingredients in a food processor or blender. Go light on the salt and pepper. Process or pulse to your liking. You want it well mixed. Chill.

Salad

Shave and slice cucumber and place it in a salad bowl. Add tomatoes, cored and sliced. Thinly slice red onion or shallot, and add it to the bowl. Toss together, then top with feta cheese. Add more or less cheese, to taste. Chill in the refrigerator, and toss with homemade Dijon Salad Dressing just before serving.

Dijon Salad Dressing

In a small bowl, whisk together the lemon juice, Dijon mustard, champagne vinegar, and salt and pepper (start with ¼ teaspoon each of salt and pepper, and adjust from there). Slowly add the olive oil while whisking the dressing, and continue to whisk vigorously to emulsify to your desired consistency. Add a bit of freshly cut oregano and let the dressing chill. Dress the salad just before serving.

Pacific Cod
Ceviche with Mango

DIRECTIONS

Preheat the broiler. Shuck the corn, drizzle it with olive oil, sprinkle it with salt and pepper, and place it on a baking pan. Broil it about 15 minutes or until roasted to your preference, shaking the pan every 4 or 5 minutes to get an even roast.

Chop, slice, and dice everything else, from the cod to the avocado. Everything should be fairly uniform in size, up to about ¼-inch pieces. Add everything to a large bowl or a gallon-size resealable plastic bag.

Allow the corn to cool a bit, then slice the kernels off the cob and add them to the bowl or plastic bag with the fish mixture.

Add the lime juice to the mixture, and let the blend marinate in the refrigerator for at least 45 minutes or up to 2 hours. This lets the fish "cook" in the lime juice.

Spread a thin layer of mayo on one side of each tostada and top it with the ceviche.

Note: I don't use any serrano peppers or cherry peppers, which is what lots of people enjoy. The kids aren't into the heat, and so I add some candied jalapeños to my plate alone and it is perfect!

★ Serves 6 ★

INGREDIENTS

2 ears fresh corn

2 to 3 T. olive oil

Salt and pepper, to taste

1 to 1½ lbs. Pacific cod fillet

1 pint cherry tomatoes

1 purple onion

3 to 4 garlic cloves

1 bunch cilantro

1 cucumber

1 mango

1 avocado

4 limes, juiced

Tostadas

Mayonnaise

Candied jalapeño (optional)

> **NOTE:** With ceviche you are not cooking the fish over heat, but it is the acidity from the citrus that is "cooking" the fish.

Traditional Shrimp Scampi

INGREDIENTS

1 lb. linguini pasta

2 T. butter

2 T. extra-virgin olive oil

4 garlic cloves, minced

1 shallot, finely diced

½ cup dry white wine

1 pinch red pepper flakes

1 lb. large shrimp, peeled and deveined

1 lemon, juiced

¼ cup chopped fresh parsley

Salt and pepper, to taste

DIRECTIONS

Bring a pot of lightly salted water to a boil over medium heat, cook the linguini to al dente according to package directions, and drain.

Melt the butter and olive oil in a large skillet over medium heat. Add the garlic and shallot and cook until fragrant. Then add the wine and red pepper flakes and cook for 30 seconds. Now add the shrimp and sauté for just a few minutes; turn them pink but don't overdo it. About 3 to 5 minutes should be enough. Remove the pan from the heat, add the lemon juice, parsley, salt, and pepper, and serve immediately over the linguini. Perhaps a crispy baguette would help sop up what's left in the pan!

★ Serves 4 ★

Grandy's Scallop Risotto with Herb Pesto

This risotto pairs well with most proteins. Scallops, a side of dressed microgreens, and a good chardonnay are so much fun with this. It's great to recruit a little help when making this dish, so that everything can finish at the same time.

DIRECTIONS

Prepare the corn and bacon: Heat the oven to 400°. Leave the corn in the husk and soak it for 30 minutes, then roast it for 20 minutes. When the corn is out of the oven, peel off the husks and shave the kernels from cob. Cook the bacon either in the oven with the corn or on the stovetop. Keep an eye on it and cook until crisp, then remove from heat, set on paper towels to drain grease if needed, and dice into bits. Set these both aside to keep warm.

Meanwhile, heat the stock in a small saucepan over medium heat.

Make a soffritto of the onion, celery and garlic: In a deep skillet or Dutch oven, heat 2 tablespoons of the olive oil with 2 tablespoons of the butter. When the butter is melted, add the vegetables and cook on low for 10 to 12 minutes to soften.

Increase the heat to medium and add the rice to the soffritto. Fry the rice, stirring constantly, for 1 to 2 minutes. Stir in the wine and keep stirring until the rice has absorbed the wine. Add one cup of the hot stock and a little salt. Reduce the heat to a simmer and continue to stir as the rice absorbs the stock. Keep adding stock, one cup at a time, once each amount is absorbed into the rice. Take your time with this process. It could take around 20 minutes to accomplish the creamy consistency and doneness desired of the rice. Do a taste test to be sure the rice is at the right texture and the seasoning is right. Adjust the salt level or cooking time as needed.

INGREDIENTS

4 ears fresh corn, still in husk

½ lb. applewood smoked bacon

4 cups chicken or vegetable stock (I prefer homemade, organic stock) or water

1 large white onion, finely diced

3 ribs celery, finely diced

3 to 4 cloves garlic, minced

2 T. extra-virgin olive oil

5 T. butter, cubed and divided

2 cups arborio rice (I prefer Roland brand)

⅔ cup dry white wine, such as chardonnay

Salt, to taste

1½ cups quality Parmesan cheese

Fresh chives, diced, to taste

Herb Pesto (page 98)

Sea Scallops (page 98)

Remove the risotto from the heat and stir in the remaining cubes of butter and all the Parmesan. Stir to combine, then cover the pan and allow the risotto to rest for 2 minutes or so.

Stir in the roasted corn kernels, diced bacon, and fresh chives.

Plate the risotto, adding a few cooked sea scallops and a drizzle of herb pesto to each plate.

★ **Serves 4** ★

Herb Pesto

Herb Pesto

2 cups fresh, packed basil leaves, or mixed greens

½ cup freshly grated Parmesan cheese

½ cup extra-virgin olive oil

⅓ cup toasted almonds or walnuts

3 cloves garlic, minced

Salt and pepper, to taste

Pinch toasted ground fennel (optional)

Instead of just basil, you can use any combination of basil, mint, arugula, and spinach leaves. Also, pine nuts are traditional for pesto, but I don't like them as much and they are expensive, so I use almonds or walnuts.

Add all ingredients to the bowl of a food processor. Start with a pinch of pepper and ½ teaspoon salt and adjust to taste. The tiniest hint of toasted ground fennel is awesome but not necessary. Secure the lid and pulse until you're happy with the texture. Taste and adjust seasoning. A splash of lemon juice or a bit more salt will help if there is a slight bitter taste.

Sea Scallops

Sea Scallops

½ lb. dry sea scallops, thawed if frozen

Salt and pepper, to taste

1 T. canola oil or avocado oil

2 T. butter, room temperature

Pat the scallops dry with a paper towel and sprinkle them with salt and pepper. Then heat up the oil in a skillet over medium-high heat. Make sure the skillet is fully preheated. Add the scallops, spacing them evenly, and allow them to begin to brown and crisp. Add the butter to the pan and flip the scallops. This goes very quickly: about 2 minutes on one side and 1 or 2 minutes on the other side. You want the top and bottom to be brown and the center to be opaque. The butter should be soft when added so it melts quickly. Spoon the butter over the scallops, and serve immediately.

NOTE: "Dry" scallops have never been treated with any added preservatives and are immediately frozen if they are shipped. They will have a lower water content when thawed, which is much better for searing, and they will also have a better taste. But even "dry" scallops need to be pat dry for the best sear!

4

JESUS EATS WITH SINNERS:

The Table of Friendship

I met my wife at a punk rock/hardcore show in Birmingham, Alabama. Amid heavy guitar break-downs, my friends running around like maniacs, and all the screaming chaos, I noticed Jana. She wore a black T-shirt and a blue bandanna around her head and had the cutest gauged earrings. I was instantly in love with her. After the show, I mustered the strength to walk over to her and introduce myself. A few years later, in 2004, we were married. Though there's been plenty of hoopla and celebration over the twenty years that are behind us, we, like everyone who somehow stays married in this crazy world, have scraped through by the skin of our teeth on more than one occasion. Our marriage has covered the spectrum of close-ness and friendship, indifference, passing like two ships in the night, completely shipwrecked, and back to love again.

In our younger, incredibly naive, super self-righteous days, we didn't understand how people divorce one another. We would think, "Why didn't they just try harder and work it out?" (As if that has never occurred to anyone!) Yet, after being seasoned by life's battles and hardships, we get it, and it honestly makes a lot of sense why people sometimes go their separate ways. It's not like anyone ever wanted a broken heart. In our forties, we have a lot of grace in our hearts for those who have weathered the hell of divorce. My friend Levi the Poet says, "Life tends to beat the binaries out of you." He's right.

St. Luke writes, "This man receives sinners and eats with them" (Luke 15:2). Were it not for Jesus's hospitality and welcome reception of sinners like me and Jana, our marriage, faith, and life would've crumbled. I mean that with everything in me. But unfortunately, such a saying about Jesus was used by his opponents as a slur on his character. How they rolled their eyes at this so-called Messiah! According to them, he was the furthest thing from kosher. You see, cleanliness was not only about avoiding the wrong kinds of food (like shellfish and pork); cleanliness also had to do with the company one kept, yet "Tax collectors and sinners were all drawing near to hear him" (Luke 15:1).

In the first-century Jewish social context, honor was prized, and shame was despised. Tax collectors were among the most shameful and, therefore, hated. The hatred was fueled by the fact that to become a tax collector, one would have to outbid others to secure the job; from there, they would spend their lives betraying the nation of Israel, working for Rome, and overtaxing the Jewish people. Tax collectors made life way harder than it had to be. Thus they were *hated* and could keep company only with fellow traitors.

Luke also tells us that "sinners" were drawing near to Jesus. To be labeled a sinner was to be assigned a particular social class. In this setting, there were insiders and outsiders, clean and unclean, righteous and unrighteous, upright and sinners. To belong to the class of sinners implied that one was outside the bounds of the love, favor, and mercy of God. Outside, unwanted, discarded. The dumpster fire title of *sinner* paired perfectly with the inward belief of being nothing more than a religious sewer, a spiritual wasteland. Yet these outcast, unclean, good-for-nothing people were "drawing near" to hear Jesus. Why? Because he had a reputation for *dining* with the ragamuffins of society.

The Dinner Table Is a Table of Fellowship

Contrary to what some think, Jesus did not just preach judgment to sinners, teach people to hold doors for the elderly, and practice being cordial and polite. Jesus paid no regard to playing it safe, saving face, and not rocking the boat. Instead, he came to revolutionize the world by inviting us to become wholly human in the Holy Spirit—ferociously joyful citizens of the Kingdom of God. He came to completely overthrow every single traditional, social, cultural, and religious boundary that told people, "God only accepts those who clean their act up and keep their elbows off the table."

Jesus broke bread with broken people without any concern about his reputation among the religious elite. One theologian writes,

> It would be difficult to overestimate the importance of table fellowship for the cultures of the Mediterranean basin in the first century of our era. Mealtimes were far more than occasions for individuals to consume nourishment. Being welcomed at a table to eat food with another person had become a ceremony richly symbolic of friendship, intimacy, and unity.[1]

Friendship, intimacy, and unity were hardly words tax collectors and sinners thought to use in relation to God, and yet because Jesus was so deeply committed to revealing the loving, welcoming, hospitable heart of God, he took the time to welcome people "as they were not as they should be," as Brennan Manning often said.[2]

Our society is starving to death for the barrier-breaking, warm heart of Jesus. We've become so crippled by fear and convenience that we've drifted toward homogeneity and now spend time *only* with people who think like us, talk like us, vote like us, and so on. After years of sequestering ourselves, drawing lines, and reinforcing our preconceived ideas, we must pause and ask, "Are we actually becoming the society we all idealize?" The answer is no. We're becoming less creative, less loving, less accepting. We're as violent, intolerant, and judgmental as we've ever been, all in the name of progress. How do we maintain peaceable relationships among those with whom we strongly disagree? Is this not the question we're trying to answer through our marching (or not marching), posting (or not posting), and voting (or not voting)?

There's no shortage of topics tearing us apart right now. Gun control, gender politics, global warming, refugees, the water crisis, critical race theory, depletion of fossil fuels, unhoused neighbors, and abortion are just a few issues that come to mind. Yet the sinless, holy, perfect Son of God maintained relationships with people who were very different from him; he *still does*! So, what is the church, after all? It's not a country club for folks who've convinced themselves that they have it all figured out. Quite the contrary! It's a conglomeration of people that need saving, correcting, and helping. The only way into God's family is to admit that, spiritually speaking, you're bankrupt. The church is a collection of people who are unlike Jesus but who love Jesus and want to be like Jesus but can't be like Jesus without the help of Jesus through the Holy Spirit. There is literally nobody in the entire history of the church that has ever thought exactly like Jesus.

Love Is Patient

So how did Jesus do it? How did he go about living his life and maintaining friendships with people who excelled in breaking the commandments? Through the Holy Spirit, who enabled him to perfectly embody the love and truth of God. Some thirty years after Jesus ascended to heaven, St. Paul wrote, "Love is patient, love is kind. It does not envy, it does not boast, it is not proud. It does not dishonor others, it is not self-seeking, it is not easily angered, it keeps no record of wrongs. Love does not delight in evil but rejoices with the truth. It always protects, always trusts, always hopes, always perseveres. Love never fails" (1 Corinthians 13:4-8 NIV).

Jesus maintained relationships with people who were very different from him because love is not coercive but *patient*. This does not mean that Jesus affirmed everything, every idea, and every person in the world. Instead, he disagreed with people and called people to repent and change. In the case of the "rich young ruler," Jesus told him what was required to faithfully follow God and inherit eternal life. "At this the man's face fell. He went away sad, because he had great wealth" (Mark 10:22 NIV). Yet we do not read, "But then Jesus ran after him and changed his mind, relaxing the requirements for obedience." Instead, Jesus simply let him walk away. Love is patient.

There was another occasion, in John's Gospel, when Jesus said to a large crowd, "Unless you eat the flesh of the Son of Man and drink his blood, you have no life in you" (6:53). Jesus was making it explicitly clear that to follow him would involve a life of radical self-denial and exclusive allegiance to him. The crowd began to walk away, saying, "This is too much." But, again, in the moment, he didn't run down the masses and change the radical nature of his message. He simply looked over at the disciples and said, "Do you want to go away as well?" (John 6:67). Love is not self-seeking.

While Jesus did preach to the crowds, he communicated that truth and love of God in the context of relationships that went beyond a lecture hall, the local marketplace, or the synagogue. He found his way into homes where wine was poured and food was prepared, where hours could be spent talking, thinking, and challenging people around the table. The dining table can be one of the most disarming places in the world.

Consider what it would look like for you to mix it up a bit and invite a person, a couple, a family, or a group of people into your home that you may disagree with on particular topics in politics or religion and simply get to know them—not as talking points but as people, fellow image bearers of God, who, like you, need the love, mercy, grace, and kindness of the Creator. Receive them into your home with no qualifications. See what an evening of not only saying "grace" but *extending grace* could look like. It may just change everything.

QUESTIONS TO CONSIDER

What would it look like to follow Jesus in this aspect of your life? Are there already people coming to mind who you could extend grace to by inviting them in for a meal? How can you make room at your table?

Chicken

The parable of the prodigal son teaches us that there are two ways to keep our distance from God: one is through rebellion, and the other is through a kind of duty-bound heartless "obedience." To my regret, in my early adult years as a follower of Christ, I was quite self-righteous. One of the ways this manifested so clearly was around the table. Such was also common in Jesus and Paul's day. We religious folks get very uptight about both who is seated around the table and what is being served. While having tremendous respect for my teetotaling friends and family, I honestly thought that my vegan lifestyle and abstinence from alcohol somehow contributed toward my right standing before God. When I'd see a family out to eat dinner and the parents would have beer or wine at the table, I'd secretly judge them harshly.

Paul instructs us, "whether you eat or drink, or whatever you do, do all to the glory of God" (1 Corinthians 10:31). This approach is a far more thoughtful and intentional way to practice being a disciple of Jesus. It's a diet that is much more broad in scope yet it is not an irresponsible approach toward food, either. All of that to say, yes, we have our liberties to eat. We are equally free to abstain, knowing that ultimately our righteousness is in Jesus and this reality affects our daily diet. So without further ado, here are a few of my favorite dishes.

Many of the dishes in this section are straightforward things that can be done on just about any given weeknight. A couple of these are better to wait for a weekend when you've got a little more time both to cook and to *host* (the Coca-Cola BBQ Chicken and Memphis Slaw Sliders are perfect when you have a couple of extra people at the table).

Braised Chicken with Mushroom White Wine Sauce and Prosciutto

DIRECTIONS

Preheat the oven to 375°. Line a baking sheet with parchment paper and lay out room-temperature prosciutto (make sure they're spaced evenly on the baking sheet). Bake for about 10 minutes and then remove the pan from the oven and use tongs to transfer the prosciutto to a cooling rack.

Pat dry the chicken thighs with a paper towel and then sprinkle salt and pepper on both sides. Add the olive oil to a braiser or large pan with high sides. Set the heat to medium high. When the pan is preheated, brown the chicken on both sides. Then pull the chicken and set it on a plate lined with paper towels, leaving the fat and oil in the pan.

Add the onion and mushrooms to the pan, sprinkle in the oregano, and sauté for about 5 to 7 minutes, allowing them to break down nicely. Then add the wine and heavy cream and stir well.

Turn the heat to medium low, slice up the chicken, and add it back to the braiser to finish cooking. This should only take about 2 more minutes.

Crumble the prosciutto and sprinkle it into the braiser, then remove the pan from the heat.

Serve over rice and top with the parsley.

★ Serves 4 ★

INGREDIENTS

4 oz. prosciutto

4 boneless, skinless chicken thighs

1 tsp. salt

1 tsp. pepper

4 oz. olive oil

1 yellow onion, thinly sliced

8 oz. baby bella mushrooms, sliced

3 to 4 tsp. chopped fresh oregano

9 to 10 oz. white wine (like white zinfandel)

1 cup heavy cream

Cooked rice, to serve

3 T. chopped fresh parsley, to garnish

CHICKEN

Slow-Cooker Coca-Cola BBQ Chicken and Memphis Slaw Sliders

This slaw is fantastic and is well-known by many all over the South. It goes great on these sliders or as a side for another summer BBQ dish. This Coca-Cola BBQ sauce is pretty special to our family given that we're Atlanta natives. The nostalgic Coca-Cola ads really do live up to their promise; at least they have for the Earlys. As kids—long, long before I started taking my own kids to the Colman Pool here in Seattle with Cokes in tow—my brother, cousins, and I would load up a small cooler at my grandparents' house and walk to the neighborhood pool in the summers. We'd swim, dive, play, and annoy the lifeguards from sunup to sundown, only stopping for a quick sandwich and a "Coke." For those who are unfamiliar with the South, all sodas and pops are known as "Coke." We called our dad "Pops" which distinguished him from the fizzy drink. If you happen to go into a restaurant and order a soda, don't be too surprised if the server looks at you and asks "What kind of Coke would you like?" You'll need to be prepared with a specific answer of exactly what kind of soda you want. If the server replies, "We only serve Pepsi products here" it's entirely appropriate to just ask for water. Taste and loyalty win out every time.

My dad, William, was honored to work for Coca-Cola in the last few years of his life. He loved that company with all his heart. In fact, even though we were from Atlanta, we'd frequent the Coke museum. Years and years ago, my grandmother, MaMa, cut this recipe for "Coca-Cola BBQ Sauce" out of the *Atlanta Journal-Constitution* and mailed it to my brother. He shared it with me and so now it's being revived here in Seattle so as to make sure it never loses its place!

DIRECTIONS

For the BBQ sauce, heat the vegetable oil in a saucepan over medium heat and sauté the onion and garlic until tender, about 8 minutes. Mix in the rest of the ingredients, stirring well until the sauce is combined. If you don't use it all for this meal, it keeps well in the refrigerator.

For the chicken, add the breasts to the slow cooker and set to high. Combine the remaining ingredients in a bowl, mix it well, then add the seasoning blend to the slow cooker on top of the chicken. Allow the chicken to cook for 3 to 4 hours. When finished, shred it with two forks.

While the chicken is cooking, make the Memphis Slaw. Simply combine all the ingredients in a bowl, mix it well, cover, and place it in the refrigerator until time to eat.

Serve on buns, topped with BBQ sauce.

★ Serves 6 ★

INGREDIENTS

BBQ Sauce

3 T. vegetable oil

1 cup minced yellow onion

4 cloves minced garlic

1 (12 oz.) can Coca-Cola

1½ cups ketchup

¼ cup apple cider vinegar

¼ cup Worcestershire sauce

1 tsp. chili powder

Hot pepper sauce (optional)

Salt and pepper, to taste

Chicken

3 lbs. boneless, skinless chicken breasts

1 onion, chopped

6 cloves garlic, minced

⅓ cup honey

1 T. oregano

1 T. Dijon mustard

1 tsp. smoked paprika

½ tsp. ground cumin

Memphis Slaw

1 (16 oz.) bag green cabbage coleslaw mix

1 to 2 shredded carrots

1 bunch cilantro, chopped

1 cup mayonnaise

2 T. Dijon mustard

1 T. honey

1 tsp. onion powder

1 tsp. celery seeds

Serve

6 slider buns

RACIAL RECONCILIATION AROUND THE TABLE

The highlight of my week rolls around every Thursday morning at 10:00 a.m. That's when my friend Katie joins me at University House (UH) here in Seattle to love and serve some of the greatest people in the world. UH is an absolutely beautiful assisted-living center for senior citizens. The cleanliness, artwork, staff, dining, and accommodations are the nicest I've ever seen in such a facility. A few years ago, a couple in our church, Bob and Elsie, asked me if I'd be interested in starting a Bible study for them and anyone else at UH that might be interested. Over the years our relationships have grown, and the nature of the group has evolved as discussions have revolved around various subjects from Scripture and politics to reading and discussing authors such as Tolstoy!

Our precious friends that join every week come from all kinds of ethnic and religious backgrounds. Let me tell you, when you gather a Jewish woman whose family did not survive Auschwitz, a Buddhist, an agnostic, an Anglican, some Catholics, and a few Protestants—all in the last chapter of life—to discuss truth, beauty, meaning, values, and ethics, the conversations are never dull! Katie and I walk out of there every single week talking about how precious each of our friends is and how much we learn from them. Each person brings a unique perspective, one informed not so much by Twitter or what's in the news, but by living over eight decades, raising families, and traveling the world. Their kindness and wisdom is more than helpful, especially living in times of such radical division at every corner in our society.

Our friend Lily shared one of the most wonderful stories about racial reconciliation, grace, and lunch. Lily is a beautiful Filipino woman who deeply loves Jesus and has belonged to the Catholic Church her entire life. Her faith is more than inspiring; it's beautiful. Some of her family members were captured and placed into Japanese internment camps during World War II. Her father escaped, and they made their long journey to Seattle. When they arrived, Lily, a kindergartner, was enrolled in school. On her first day of school, she was understandably quite nervous. She was equally worried about encountering Japanese classmates. "Oh, Lord, what will I do if I have to sit near a Japanese child? How will they treat me? Help me, Lord," she prayed. In God's providence, a little Japanese girl came into the classroom and sat at the desk in front of Lily. Her heart raced and her anxiety went up as she thought, "What will happen today?"

Finally, it was lunchtime. The little Japanese girl turned around, met Lily's gaze, and said, "Hi! I'm Vicky! Would you like to share my lunch with me?" The walls came down that day as they ate crisp Washington apple slices together, and now, decades later, Vicky and Lily are still best friends.

Open your heart. Look around. Who could you share an apple with today?

Lime Chicken Tenders with Coconut Basil Rice and Pickled Cucumbers

INGREDIENTS

2¼ lbs. boneless chicken tenders

Marinade

½ cup soy sauce

2 to 3 T. oyster sauce or fish sauce

4 limes, juiced

3 to 4 T. minced garlic

1 to 2 T. grated fresh ginger

1 to 2 tsp. red pepper flakes

Cucumbers

1 English cucumber

1 cup rice vinegar

2 limes, juiced

Red pepper flakes (optional)

Coconut Basil Rice

13 to 14 oz. unsweetened coconut milk

1½ cups water

2 cups jasmine rice

1 lime, zested and juiced

2 T. fresh basil, chopped

Optional toppings

Soft-boiled eggs

Sriracha

KariKari garlic chili crisp

DIRECTIONS

Place the chicken tenders in a gallon-size resealable plastic bag. Whisk together all marinade ingredients in a bowl, then pour the mixture over the chicken in the bag. Seal the bag and place it in the refrigerator for at least an hour.

Thinly slice the cucumbers with a box grater or mandoline and place them in a bowl. Add the vinegar and lime juice, and sprinkle the cucumbers with red pepper flakes if desired. Stir gently, then cover the bowl and place it in the refrigerator to chill.

Start the rice (instructions below) after the chicken has been marinating for about 45 minutes.

To cook the chicken, preheat your grill to 425°. Use tongs and lay out the chicken tenders on the grate and cook for 8 to 12 minutes. The chicken is done when it has reached an internal temperature of 165°.

I like to serve this dish in bowls with rice on one side of the bowl, cucumbers on the other, and chicken on top. This goes great with a soft-boiled egg and some sriracha if that's your style—or even better, KariKari garlic chili crisp.

★ Serves 4 ★

Coconut Basil Rice

In a medium saucepan, bring coconut milk and water to a boil over medium heat, stirring often. Stir in rice, cover, and simmer on low until the rice is tender and the liquid has been absorbed, about 15 minutes. Stir in the lime zest and juice when the rice is nearly finished. Stir in basil just before serving.

"Let It Eat!" Sheet-Pan Chicken and Veggies with Boss Sauce

Jana and I started dating at a punk rock and hardcore music festival called Furnace Fest back in the year 2000. The festival is so named because it is held in the historic Sloss Furnaces in Birmingham, Alabama. You'll have to look this place up! On that great day when I pledged my true love for Jana, I also met my beloved friend, Johnny Alan Grimes II. He's a brother who has stood by me through thick and thin and makes me one of the wealthiest people in the world because our relationship is invaluable. He and a few buddies resurrected the indescribable Furnace Fest, and he's in the midst of a crew known as the Sloss Boyz; my family. This sheet-pan chicken is in honor of Johnny Grimes, Lee Early, Chesley McCormick, John Anderson, Dax Bone, Don Clark, Kirk Castro, and Rob Stoots. Let it eat, boys!

DIRECTIONS

Mix together all the marinade ingredients and marinate the chicken overnight.

Preheat the oven to 425°.

Place the chicken onto the sheet pan and surround it with all the cut veggies. Drizzle olive oil lightly over all the veggies. Bake for about 20 minutes, keeping an eye on the chicken, watching for it to crisp up a bit.

While the chicken and veggies are baking, make the Boss Sauce.

Right after removing the chicken and veggies from the oven, drizzle the sauce over everything on the pan, and serve. The amount of flavor that comes through this Mongolian-influenced marinade with all the veggies and mustard sauce is simply mind-blowing!

★ Serves 4 ★

INGREDIENTS

1 to 1½ lbs. chicken thighs, bone in and skin on

Marinade

1 cup hoisin sauce

1 scallion, white and two-thirds of the green parts, minced

¼ cup minced fresh cilantro, leaves and stems

1½ T. minced garlic

1½ T. dark soy sauce

1½ T. sherry vinegar

1½ T. rice vinegar

1 T. sugar

1 T. white miso

1½ tsp. peeled and grated fresh ginger

1 tsp. Tabasco sauce

¾ tsp. white pepper

1 T. sesame oil

Veggies

1 (24 oz.) bag baby potato medley

10 to 12 brussels sprouts, chopped in half

5 radishes, thinly sliced

2 fennel bulbs, greens removed and white ends thinly sliced

2 carrots, thinly sliced

1 yellow onion, thinly sliced

1 to 2 T. olive oil

Boss Sauce (page 118)

Boss Sauce

½ cup sugar

¼ cup Colman's mustard
  powder

2 egg yolks

½ cup red wine vinegar

¾ cup crème fraîche

Boss Sauce (Chinese-Style Mustard Sauce)

Prepare a double boiler with water in the lower part and heat it to a simmer. In the top of the double boiler, whisk together sugar with mustard powder. When well combined, whisk in egg yolks and vinegar. Cook the sauce over simmering water in the double boiler, stirring occasionally, for 10 to 15 minutes, until it is thick enough to form ribbons when drizzled from the spoon. Turn off the heat and remove the top part of the pan to allow the mixture to cool.

When it is cool, fold in crème fraîche. If you will not be using this right away, keep it refrigerated until needed.

★ **Makes about 2 cups** ★

Chicken Boats
with Thai Peanut Sauce

DIRECTIONS

Prepare the rice and peanut sauce, then preheat a charcoal grill to 400°.

Mix the seasonings together in a small bowl. Drizzle both sides of the chicken with olive oil and sprinkle both sides evenly with the spices. Then head to the grill. Place the chicken on the grate and grill for about 5 minutes on each side. The internal temperature should reach 165°. When it's fully cooked, remove the chicken from the grill, place it on a cutting board, and chop it into small cubes.

To assemble, take a romaine heart to use as your boat. Add a couple spoonfuls of the coconut rice to the boat and spread it around. Top the rice with chicken, followed by peanut sauce, and then finally the pomegranate arils.

★ Serves 4 ★

Thai Peanut Sauce

Toast the peanuts in a dry skillet over medium heat until they give a nice fragrance, about 1 to 2 minutes. Remove and set aside. Keeping the stove set to medium, heat the peanut oil in the skillet. Add the curry paste and cook for about a minute. Then add the remaining ingredients. Stir well and reduce heat. Allow the sauce to thicken and simmer for a few minutes, adjusting the heat as necessary.

TIPS FOR GRILLING CHICKEN: One thing that helps me achieve even cooking when I'm grilling chicken breasts is to put a ⅛-inch-deep slit into the chicken breast about every ¼ inch. (Do this before adding any seasoning to the chicken.) This allows me to keep a close eye on how everything is cooking. The worst thing is to think you're finished by judging the outside of a chicken breast, only to cut into it and realize there's still work to be done. With the cuts in the chicken breast, you can monitor the cooking for yourself. That's how I've done it for years. Others prefer to use a meat thermometer. If that's you, you'll always want the chicken's internal temperature to reach 165°.

INGREDIENTS

1 head romaine lettuce, washed and separated into large leaves

Chicken

2 boneless, skinless chicken breasts (about 1 lb.)

4 T. olive oil

½ tsp. salt

½ tsp. pepper

1 tsp. ground cumin

1 tsp. smoked paprika

Coconut Basil Rice (page 114)

Thai Peanut Sauce

2 T. chopped peanuts

1 T. peanut oil

1 T. red curry paste

¼ cup peanut butter

½ cup coconut milk

3 T. fish sauce

2 T. lime juice

2 T. brown sugar

1 T. sriracha (or to taste)

Serve

1 cup pomegranate arils

"TASTE AND SEE"

As we savor the goodness in a meal and appreciate the subtle flavors and essences in a good drink, the dining experience can be one way in which we really feel human together. One of my favorite things to do for a group of my friends is to go to the grocery early in the morning and ask the butcher to cut a few one-inch rib eyes, keeping a keen eye out for the right amount of marbling. I'll then prepare the marinade for the evening's Hawaiian Rib Eye feast. It's a quick marinade provided by Houston's Steakhouse, first introduced to me and tweaked just a bit by my dear friend, Walt Sellers. I call him my "Papa Walt" (P.W.). He and his beloved bride, Sharon (Dr. Sellers) are invaluable friends to me and Jana.

Back in 2008, I was busy planting Four Corners Church in Newnan, Georgia. I worked in a bar called The Alamo, and the church met at the same bar on Sunday mornings. P.W. and Dr. Sellers began attending shortly after my father passed away in March 2009. They quickly embraced Jana and I as their own children, and we've been close ever since. Because of space limitations, I cannot go into just how much the Sellers mean to me; you'll just have to come over some time and get the story straight from the Earlys.

Back to the steak: This rib eye is one that we all love, and all day long we eagerly anticipate both the steak and the smiles that are soon to fill the kitchen. The rib eyes are drenched in a delicious brown-sugary, pineapple-juicy, vinegary, soy, gingery, garlicky goodness for a few hours. Though steak tends to be eaten with a fork and knife and table cloth, we prefer to dine like kids with our fingers for this one.

As friends arrive, our children run wild, music plays loudly, and all the hugs, laughs, and exclamations of "Hey! How are ya?" quickly fill the kitchen and spill out into the yard. We light the charcoal grill and throw the rib eyes on, cooking them to perfection (medium rare with a nice sear). When it's time to pull the steaks from the grill, we let them rest for just a few moments, and the aroma fills the kitchen. Finally, we lay the steaks out on the big cutting board and cut them all up into basically long strips of finger food. Then we stand around eating rib eyes with our fingers. Right then, in that moment, we're not only laughing and savoring everything—we're savoring being with each other. There's life in the kitchen because that's where your family and friends are. It is there that our trust, love, and appreciation for one another grow. We feel at home. We're together. We can taste and see that the Lord is good and, by his grace, so are we. Amen.

Chicken Piccata
with Crispy Capers

DIRECTIONS

First, prepare the crispy capers. Pour about 4 tablespoons of olive oil into a large pan and heat over medium-high until the oil begins to shimmer. Then add the drained capers to the oil; allow the capers to fry until they turn brown, stirring as needed. Using a slotted spoon, remove the capers and place them on a paper towel–lined plate and allow them to drain of excess oil. Leave the remaining oil in the pan, and turn off the heat while you prepare the chicken.

Pat the chicken dry with paper towels. Season the chicken lightly with salt and pepper and then dredge it in flour and place it on a plate. Add 2 tablespoons of butter to the oil in the skillet and heat over medium-high. Allow the butter to begin to brown and then place half of the chicken in the pan. Cook the chicken through on both sides. Remove the chicken, place it on a lined plate, and cover it with aluminum foil to keep warm. Add 2 tablespoons of butter and 2 tablespoons of olive oil to the skillet, melt together, then repeat the process with the rest of the chicken.

Into the same skillet, once the chicken is removed, add the shallot to the pan and allow it to start breaking down for just a minute. Then add the garlic and do the same thing. Stir in the stock and simmer, allowing it to reduce by about half. Lower the heat and add the remaining butter with the lemon juice, zest, and capers. Once all the butter has melted and the sauce is combined, add the chicken back to the pan with the crispy capers. Top with parsley. This dish can be served over fettuccini!

★ Serves 4 ★

INGREDIENTS

6 T. olive oil, divided

2 T. capers, drained

1 lb. chicken cutlets, tenders, or chicken breasts (halved horizontally)

Salt and pepper, to taste

1 cup flour for dredging

8 T. butter, cut into pieces, divided

1 shallot, thinly sliced

1 T. minced garlic

1½ cups chicken stock

1 T. lemon juice

2 tsp. lemon zest

Chopped fresh parsley, for garnish

CHICKEN

5

BREAD AND WINE: The Center of the Church

"Recipes are how we learn all the rules, and cooking is knowing how to break them to suit our tastes or preferences. Following a recipe is like playing scales and cooking is jazz."[1] On Maundy Thursday (*Maundy* is a Latin term meaning "commandment"), there was a deep tradition, a strict recipe, a meticulous scale that was expected to be played at the Passover. Yet suddenly Jesus began to break some rules and start playing jazz, something no God-fearing, devout, reverent, obedient Jew would ever think to do. In a single moment, he hijacked the ancient tradition of Passover and made it *all about himself*. The Gospel of Luke tells us,

When the hour came, Jesus and his apostles reclined at the table. And he said to them, "I have eagerly desired to eat this Passover with you before I suffer. . ." After taking the cup, he gave thanks and said, "Take this and divide it among you. . ." And he took bread, gave thanks and broke it, and gave it to them, saying, "This is my body given for you; do this in remembrance of me. . ." In the same way, after the supper he took the cup, saying, "This cup is the new covenant in my blood, which is poured out for you" (22:14-15, 17, 19-20 NIV).

The sacrament of bread and wine has many names: communion, holy eucharist, the Last Supper, the Lord's Supper. They all point to the one man, the Lord Jesus Christ, the head of the church, who loved us and gave himself for us. Broken bread and poured wine are common elements that tell the most spectacular story, the one about the God who will stop at absolutely nothing to be reunited with his wayward children. Carbohydrates and crushed grapes are telling us that the brutal death and glorious resurrection of Jesus are not add-ons to the life of the church; they are the very high point; for it is *there* that the faith in our minds and beliefs in our hearts engage the tastebuds of our tongues as we consume the covenant, the very promise of God. We behold his death and we swallow up his life.

The Point of a Church

Over eighty years ago the world was barreling toward global catastrophe. A war among the nations was now on the horizon for the second time. Men, women, boys, and girls all over the globe were all longing for a peace that only heaven can truly provide. It's in moments like this, moments of crisis, distress, and disorientation, that we naturally look to and long for leaders who will tell the truth and give us hope with clarity, conviction, and compassion. In 1941, the famed Oxford scholar, novelist, and apologist C.S. Lewis was just the man primed and ready for such an occasion.

In the evenings, he would go on BBC Radio from 7:45 to 8:00 p.m. and give a brief talk entitled "Right or Wrong: A Clue to the Meaning of the Universe." Those radio lectures were eventually compiled into the now infamous work *Mere Christianity*. Each page drips with the truth of the gospel, homing in on the essentials of the Christian faith and why Christianity makes sense even in our modern, ever-changing world. As he likens the purpose for the existence of the church and government, clarity springs to life. He writes,

> The State exists simply to promote and to protect the ordinary happiness of human beings in this life. A husband and wife

chatting over a fire, a couple of friends having a game of darts in a pub, a man reading a book in his own room or digging in his own garden—that is what the State is there for. . . The church exists for nothing else but to draw men into Christ, to make them little Christs. If they are not doing that, all the cathedrals, clergy, missions, sermons, even the Bible itself, are simply a waste of time.[2]

And all God's people said, "Amen" (as they say in the Deep South). The point of the church is to consistently magnify Jesus, through the Holy Spirit, to the glory of God the Father. That's the point.

Grounded by the Elements

Throughout the New Testament, Jesus and the apostles describe the church not as a country club, political party, or somewhere to pay dues and enjoy perks; instead it is called the bride of Christ (Ephesians 5:31-32), the body of Christ (Romans 12:4-5), the house of God (1 Timothy 3:14-15). As the bride, as we take the bread and wine we are reminded of our wedding day when we entered into an unbreakable covenant with our Groom. As the body, we are nourished by the bread and wine as the Head guides and provides for our every need. As the house of God, the bread and wine call us to attend to the indwelling Holy Spirit, who binds us together in peace. The church belongs exclusively to God, and he is *jealous* for her to know him, stay in step with him, and not stray after that which cannot satisfy. The communion elements serve to ground us in the unmovable love of God.

Because Jesus is meek and our flesh is frail, we desperately need to take of the sacrament every week. This is because the main reason for why we gather, namely Jesus himself, is easily supplanted by our focus drifting toward someone or something else, often a good thing like songs or theological education, or even serving the poor. Now, don't get me wrong—the Bible has plenty to say about singing, growing, and serving! Yet communion keeps us grounded with regard to who it is all about and why we sing, study, and serve the way we do. What's the point of gathering on Sundays for worship or home Bible studies, reading books, streaming songs, attending conferences, and downloading podcasts if we aren't being drawn into Christ the same way we are drawn toward the smells of sautéing garlic, roasting chicken thighs, and fresh-baked bread?

A Sacred Covenant

I'll never forget the first time I got a glimpse of just how holy, serious, and sacred a *covenant* really is. It was the summer of 1994. I was a fourteen-year-old boy and could not have been more in need of a wake-up call. The trajectory I was on looked pretty bleak, to say the least. I had just finished the eighth grade. I say "finished" because I technically didn't pass; I was "placed" into the ninth grade because I had failed every class except typing, which I passed by one point. The only thing worse than my grades was my behavior. I was spending one of several summers in summer school, locked away with the rest of the ragamuffins from my county. I came to discover that summer school was a little bit like the movie *The Breakfast Club*. In the movie, the assistant principal, Richard Vernon, stings the degenerate high schoolers with two sentences: "It is now 7:06. You have exactly eight hours and fifty-four minutes to think about why you are here—to ponder the error of your ways." I wish I had done more pondering.

One evening after school I was in a particularly foul mood. My brother had gone fishing with a buddy and was just coming in, happy as a clam. I still had homework to do, and on top of that, I was grounded, having already forfeited all my Nirvana CDs. My mom had made baked spaghetti. It wasn't bad; it wasn't a showstopper either. For some reason I decided to smart off to her, thinking it was just me, my brother, and her in the kitchen. Wrong. As I unleashed my frustration on my mother, I was suddenly grabbed by the arm and spun around like a top. I found myself face-to-face with my dad, who never raised his voice; he suddenly boomed, "HEY! THAT'S—MY—WIFE!" I felt the blood drain from my face as I came to recognize for the first time in my life that Bevy was not just my mom; she and my dad had made a *covenant*. My dad never raised his voice again—he didn't have to—and I don't think I ever talked back to my mom after that. Message received: covenant is about serious, holy love.

The next time you partake of the bread and wine, allow the words of the gospel to find a place in your spirit; through the elements, taste, see, and hear Jesus saying, "I love you, I am with you, I am for you." You are the bride of Christ, and he is jealous for you.

QUESTIONS TO CONSIDER

**Did you grow up going to church?
If so, what was your experience with communion?
How can you appreciate it as a covenantal
action instead of a routine or a transaction?**

Tacos and Wraps

I don't know who invented "Taco Tuesday" but I both admire the person and struggle to understand them. I celebrate this act of almighty taco justice that has set tacos apart from all other foods by designating a day for them. And while tacos are great on Tuesday, has there ever been a day in which you *didn't want tacos*? Probably not. Breakfast, second breakfast, lunch, happy hour, dinner, late night snack … I really can't think of a time I didn't want tacos. There's a few creative tacos to choose from here. As you cook these, you'll notice that there's a repeated pattern: a fried tortilla, usually a sort of spicy jam on the base, followed by a marinated protein, then topped with a slaw of some sort. Long before ever hearing of the now famous "salt, fat, acid, heat" elements of flavorful cooking, I was basically following along those lines. I think the meal I've made for more friends than any other are the shrimp tacos. Oh, and a note about the pepper jelly on the shrimp tacos must be stated here. In 2009, my friend Jon Snell and I were making shrimp tacos one afternoon. We gave one to his nine-year-old daughter, Riley (or "Rue" as we call her), and a stroke of genius came forth: "You know, these are great, but you should add some red pepper jelly to the base!" As the Bible says, "Out of the mouth of babes." And so red pepper jelly came to be the magic ingredient to shrimp tacos. Trust me. Rue was right.

I advise you to turn up *August and Everything After* by Counting Crows while you cook, sing along, feel the feelings, and serve these tacos to your family and friends. Feast until your hearts are content!

Grilled Chicken Tacos with Spicy Jalapeño Jam, Lime Cabbage, and Black Beans

DIRECTIONS

Rinse and pat dry both sides of the chicken thighs with paper towels, then place them in a bowl. Add the seasoning rub ingredients to a small bowl in the order listed and mix well. Rub this seasoning blend on the chicken thighs. Cover the chicken thighs and leave them in the refrigerator until it is time to grill, at least 20 minutes.

Thinly slice the green cabbage and place it in a large bowl. Add the carrot, lime juice, and celery seed, and stir well.

Preheat the grill to 375°, then grill the chicken thighs for about 4 minutes per side, flipping once midway through cooking. The chicken needs to be at least 165° to make sure it's cooked properly. You can use a meat thermometer to check. Remove the chicken from the grill and slice it into bite-size pieces.

Serve

Fry your tortillas when the chicken is just about ready. Spread up to 1 tablespoon jalapeño jam on the base of the taco, pile on chicken, then cabbage, and top with cotija cheese and black beans.

★ Serves 4 ★

Tortillas

For a *good* tortilla, right before assembly, simply warm the tortillas in the microwave for 60 seconds.

For an *amazing* tortilla, heat about ½ inch of canola oil in a skillet on medium-high. Toss in one tortilla at a time, leaving them in place in the oil until they start to blow up a bit. Fry on both sides. It doesn't take long, maybe 15 to 30 seconds, so they are still pliable, but the light frying opens up a shocking amount of flavor. Use tongs to remove the hot tortilla from the oil, place it on a tray, and salt the hot tortilla ever so slightly. Repeat the process with all the tortillas, covering the cooked ones to keep them warm as you go. Then you're ready to build your masterpiece.

INGREDIENTS

4 boneless, skinless chicken thighs

Seasoning Rub

2 limes, juiced

1 tsp. ground cumin

1 tsp. paprika

4 garlic cloves, minced

1 T. ancho chili or traditional Mexican chili powder

½ to 1 cup chopped fresh cilantro

¼ cup olive oil

1 tsp. salt

1 tsp. pepper

Lime Cabbage

½ head green cabbage

1 carrot, julienned

2 limes, juiced

1 tsp. celery seed

Tortillas

12 (6-inch) flour tortillas, warmed or fried

Canola oil

Salt, to taste

Serve

Jalapeño jam (I use Inna Jam Plenty Spicy Jalapeño Jam)

Cotija cheese, crumbled

Black beans, cooked

INGREDIENTS

1½ lbs. skirt steak

Marinade

¾ cup sodium-free soy sauce

2 T. honey

2 tsp. red pepper flakes

2 T. diced fresh ginger

2 T. minced fresh garlic

Sour Cucumber Radish Slaw

1 English cucumber

4 red radishes

5 T. rice wine vinegar

1 tsp. red pepper flakes

Corn

2 ears fresh corn

4 T. olive oil

Salt and pepper, to taste

1½ to 2 T. Kewpie (Japanese mayonnaise)

1 T. Mexican hot chili powder

6-inch flour tortillas, warmed or fried (page 135)

Serve

Laoganma chili crisp (you can find this in any Asian grocery, and it is often also available in other groceries among the Asian foods)

Hot sauce (I use Heartbeat Hot Sauce by Heatonis)

Chili Crunch Steak Tacos with Sour Cucumber Radish Slaw and Corn

DIRECTIONS

Steak

Place the steaks in the bottom of a big bowl. Mix the marinade ingredients together in a small bowl and pour it over the meat. Allow the meat to marinate for 2 hours. Heat the grill to about 550°. I love grilling the steaks over coals until medium rare (which has an internal temperature of 130° to 135°). It should take about 10 minutes. Remove the meat, allow it to rest for about 10 minutes, then thinly slice the steak into strips, and then again down to bite-size pieces.

Sour Cucumber Radish Slaw

Peel and thinly slice the cucumber and radish and place them in a medium bowl. Alternately, (and this is more fun!) use a Joseph Joseph Spiro Handheld Spiralizer to make long radish noodles. Add the rice wine vinegar and red pepper flakes to the bowl and toss with the vegetables.

Corn

Turn on the broiler to preheat while you shuck the corn. Place the ears on a baking sheet and coat with olive oil, then sprinkle lightly with salt and pepper. Broil until finished, approximately 6 to 8 minutes per side, flipping once. Remove the corn from the oven and slice the kernels off the cob (I tend to just hold the corn with some tongs and use my bread knife—I know, I know—to slice the kernels directly onto the baking sheet). Use a flat spatula to scoop the corn into a large bowl, stir in the mayonnaise, then add the Mexican chili powder and stir again.

Serve

Apply 1 tablespoon (or desired amount) of Laoganma chili crisp to the base of each flour tortilla. Add the steak, top with slaw, then corn, and finally drizzle the hot sauce over the top.

★ Serves 4 ★

MEN IN THE KITCHEN

When you were growing up, who did the majority of the grocery shopping, prepping, and cooking in your home? In the Early home, it was my mom, Bevy. Every Saturday she would head to the grocery store with her handwritten shopping list, ready to purchase all that would be needed for the coming week—knowing that my brother and I would devour everything by the following Wednesday and, thus, a midweek run to the grocery after choir practice was inevitable. Aside from all the shopping, Bevy also did all the cooking. Ernie and I would loudly come through the kitchen, grazing, drinking directly out of the milk jug, oftentimes practicing our pro-wrestling moves on each other. Not once did it occur to us to offer a helping hand to our dear mother (Lord, forgive us, for our sins are many). Bevy didn't seem to mind as she'd carry on in her labor of love.

Yet the tides are changing as several recent studies have shown that more and more men find themselves enjoying the kitchen. Kevin Curry, founder of FitMenCook, says, "It's a masculine quality to want to physically put food on the table and make it taste good."[3] I agree with Curry; as someone whose work is either at a desk or meeting with others face-to-face, I find it so rewarding to physically work with ingredients, pots, pans, and other kitchen tools, bring a meal to completion, and then place it on the table for my family and friends. Countless men are now seeing that the kitchen isn't just a utilitarian space like a garage or shed, which exists solely to get a job done. The kitchen is different. It's where family, friends, and creativity all come together. It's where life is nourished and relationships strengthened. Such work is hardly the domain of one gender, don't you think?

Shrimp Tacos with Holy Guacamole, Sanctified Slaw, and Screamin' Sour Cream

Developed over three years by Jon Snell, Grandy Streets, and Alex Early.

I mentioned my friend Jon in the introduction as the main person responsible for getting me into cooking. He loves foods that are rich, explosive, and memorable. His lifelong friend Grandy is also *quite the cook!* I've never met Grandy face to face. We've texted for years but have never cooked together. The three of us batted different ideas around with these shrimp tacos for three years and they've arrived at perfection.

DIRECTIONS

First make all the elements (pages 142 to 143), then return to this page for assembly instructions. Here are some things we've learned over the years:

1. Make the Screamin' Sour Cream first and throw it into the fridge so the flavors can get happy.
2. Then get your shrimp into the marinade and set it in the fridge for at least a half hour.
3. After that, prepare the Sanctified Slaw. You want to make the slaw early enough in the process that the flavors can marinate some, but not so far ahead that things get wilty.
4. It's a good idea to make the Holy Guacamole last for two reasons. Reason number 1, you don't want the avocado turning brown while you're cooking the other stuff, so plan to prep everything and wait until the last minute to cut open the avocados and mix them in. Reason number 2, if you make it ahead of time, you'll eat it all on chips or tortillas, or off your fingers, before the rest of the stuff is ready—and you do not want to miss having this in the shrimp tacos!
5. Finally, cook the shrimp and fry your tortillas, and start piling them up.

Assemble

Take one fried tortilla and spread a thin layer of red pepper jelly on one side. This is the *most* important ingredient. Your heart will sing songs to heaven. Next, spread a dollop of Screamin' Sour Cream on top of that. Sprinkle on some cheese, add 3 to 5 shrimp (I will sometimes cut these in half, depending on their size), and sprinkle more cheese on top. Sprinkle crushed lime tortilla chips onto the tacos for added crunch. Add a dollop of Holy Guacamole, and finish with a good spoonful of Sanctified Slaw.

Go ahead and make 2 to 3 per plate.

★ Serves 4 ★

INGREDIENTS

Fried tortillas (page 135)

Red pepper jelly (I like Stonewall Kitchen)

Shredded pepper jack cheese or a 4-cheese Mexican blend

Lime tortilla chips, crushed

Screamin' Sour Cream (page 142)

Shrimp (page 142)

Sanctified Slaw (page 142)

Holy Guacamole (page 143)

TACOS AND WRAPS

Screamin' Sour Cream

½ cup sour cream

2 tsp. hot sauce

1 tsp. garlic powder

½ tsp. salt

¼ tsp. freshly ground black pepper

Shrimp

1 lb. shrimp (30 count or so)

½ cup soy sauce

1 tsp. grated ginger

1 tsp. garlic powder

1 tsp. red pepper flakes

1 T. honey

1 T. olive oil

Salt and pepper, to taste

1 clove garlic, chopped

Sanctified Slaw

2 cups thinly sliced red cabbage

½ cup julienned or grated carrots

½ cup thinly sliced red onion

4 T. chopped fresh cilantro

4 T. rice wine vinegar

2 T. canola oil

Honey, to taste

Celery seed, to taste

Salt and pepper, to taste

Screamin' Sour Cream

In a small mixing bowl, stir together all the ingredients. Keep this in the fridge until you are ready to serve the tacos.

Shrimp

Take shrimp, peel and devein them if needed, and let them sit in this soy sauce–based marinade for up to an hour (you want the marinade to cover the shrimp, but they don't need to be swimming): Sprinkle in the soy sauce, grated ginger, garlic powder, red pepper flakes, and honey according to your own tastes, maybe starting with these amounts and adjusting from there.

When you are ready to cook the shrimp, preheat a medium-large skillet on medium heat and drizzle in about a tablespoon of olive oil. Remove the shrimp from the marinade, sprinkle with salt and pepper, and quickly sauté them in the skillet with garlic. Cook for 3 to 5 minutes, or until they are pink and opaque. They say a perfectly cooked shrimp is a "C" shape not an "O."

Sanctified Slaw

Mix the cabbage, carrots, onion, and cilantro together in a medium-large bowl. Whisk the vinegar and oil together in a small bowl (I know the vinegar-to-oil ratio generally is the other way around, but trust me that 2 vinegar to 1 oil is the way to go in this case), then drizzle it over the vegetables. Do a good spiral drizzle of honey over the top, and follow up with a good sprinkling of celery seed (it's easy to put too much celery seed, but do not go without; start with about ½ teaspoon). Sprinkle on a bit of salt and pepper (we like a lot of salt and pepper, but remember—you can always add more, but you can't take it away). Stir well to combine, then cover and refrigerate it until you are ready to eat.

Holy Guacamole

Add all ingredients to a bowl, mix well, mashing some of the avocado as you go. I think it's perfect when it's a little chunky but not so much that it competes with everything else that's going on in these tacos. Try not to immediately devour it!

Holy Guacamole

2 avocados, peeled, pitted, and chopped

1 lime, juiced

4 tsp. minced red onion

4 tsp. olive oil

2 tsp. minced fresh cilantro

2 garlic cloves, minced

½ tsp. salt

½ tsp. pepper

Short Rib Tacos with Simple Lime Slaw, Pickled Onion, and Toasted Cumin Sour Cream

This combination makes an amazing meal. The different elements are best prepared in advance so the flavors have plenty of time to meld. Start the short ribs first thing in the morning, prepare your toppings and refrigerate them, and then shred the meat and warm the tortillas (page 135) just before serving. This is perfect with a side of Mexican Street Corn (page 53).

DIRECTIONS

Pan sear your short ribs in a large skillet in butter for about a minute, then transfer them to a slow cooker. Mix the spices together in a small bowl, then sprinkle the seasoning over the short ribs. Pour the beer into the slow cooker, taking care not to wash all the spices off the meat.

Turn your slow cooker on low and let the ribs cook for 8 hours. At hour 7, turn the ribs over in the sauce one time. At the end, the meat will literally be falling off the bones. Remove the bones and shred the beef.

To assemble the tacos, warm up a pile of tortillas, layer on the beef, slaw, onion, a dollop of sour cream, and a sprinkle of cheese.

★ Serves 6 ★

Simple Lime Slaw

Place cabbage in a large bowl. Add the lime zest and juice, along with cilantro and a bit of salt. Then put it in the fridge.

Pickled Onion

Thinly slice onion and put it in a bowl. Add the lime juice along with salt, cover the bowl, and place it in the refrigerator for at least an hour.

Toasted Cumin Sour Cream

Toast cumin seeds in a dry skillet over medium heat for about 1 minute, or until the seeds are really fragrant.

Scrape the seeds into a bowl with sour cream. Add garlic powder, and stir well. Cover the bowl, place it in the refrigerator, and let the flavors meld.

INGREDIENTS

Short Ribs

3 lbs. beef short ribs

1 T. butter

1 tsp. salt

1 tsp. pepper

1 tsp. smoked paprika

1 tsp. garlic powder

1 tsp. onion powder

1 tsp. ground cumin

8 oz. beer (I use Corona or an IPA)

Simple Lime Slaw

½ small head of green cabbage, thinly sliced

1 lime, zested and juiced

¼ cup fresh cilantro, chopped

Salt, to taste

Pickled Onion

1 purple onion, sliced

6 limes, juiced (about ½ cup)

1 tsp. kosher salt

6-inch flour tortillas, warmed or fried (page 135)

Toasted Cumin Sour Cream

2 T. cumin seeds

2 cups sour cream

1 T. garlic powder

Serve

4 oz. queso fresco, crumbled

Pork Belly Tacos Two Ways

Sometimes you have to mix it up even more! Try this pork taco recipe with Watermelon Salsa on your first taco, and then put Spicy Tangy Mayo on your second taco. For an extra dash of amazing, fry the tortillas as on page 135.

DIRECTIONS

Preheat the oven to 350°.

Slice all the pork into bite-size pieces. Season with plenty of salt and pepper.

Heat the vegetable oil in a large oven-proof pan or skillet and sear the pork belly, but don't overcook it—cook just long enough to get the brown, crusted edge you're looking for.

Drain the pan of all the fat. In a small bowl, mix together the vinegar, orange juice, garlic, annatto paste, red pepper flakes, and cumin, then drizzle it over the pork in the pan. Cover the pan with aluminum foil and place it in the oven for 90 minutes. While the pork is cooking, make your Watermelon Salsa and Spicy Tangy Mayo.

After 90 minutes, remove the pork from the oven and allow it to sit (still covered) for 10 to 15 minutes to cool, and then shred it with forks, removing any remaining fat.

Warm your tortillas, then assemble. Be sure to have a couple tacos so you can try both amazing ways.

★ Serves 4 to 5 ★

Watermelon Salsa
Mix all the ingredients in a medium bowl and refrigerate until you are ready to eat.

Spicy Tangy Mayo
Mix all the ingredients in a small bowl and refrigerate until you are ready to eat.

INGREDIENTS

2 to 2½ lbs. boneless, skinless pork belly

Salt and pepper, to taste

5 T. vegetable oil

1 cup distilled white vinegar

1 cup orange juice

6 cloves garlic, minced

2 T. annatto/achiote paste (same thing!)

2 pinches red pepper flakes

¼ tsp. ground cumin

6-inch flour tortillas, warmed or fried (page 135)

Watermelon Salsa

3 cups cubed seedless watermelon

½ mango, cubed

½ cucumber, cubed

½ large red onion, minced

1 cup peeled and diced jicama

2 limes, juiced

¼ to ½ cup diced fresh cilantro

2 T. seeded and minced jalapeño (optional)

Salt, to taste

Spicy Tangy Mayo

½ cup mayonnaise

1 T. sriracha

½ lime, juiced

2 tsp. soy sauce

Pepper and garlic salt, to taste

Game Day Chicken Quesadillas with Lime Crema

DIRECTIONS

Place the chicken into a gallon-size ziplock freezer bag. Mix all the marinade ingredients in a small mixing bowl, then pour the marinade over the chicken. Marinate, refrigerated, for two hours.

To make the Lime Crema, whisk the lime juice and zest into the crema. Refrigerate until you are ready to eat.

When it's time to cook, preheat a griddle or skillet to medium-high and apply a thin layer of olive oil. Sear the chicken thighs on both sides, then let them cook all the way through. When finished, place the chicken on a cutting board and cut it into small pieces. Leave the skillet on the heat.

Take one tortilla, sprinkle on about 1 to 2 tablespoons of the Mexican blend cheese, then top with the desired amount of black beans, cotija cheese, pickled onion, Mama Lil's, chopped chicken, and finally sprinkle on a bit more Mexican blend. Place a second tortilla on top and then place each quesadilla into your skillet (or onto the griddle) and allow it to toast for about 2 minutes. Keep an eye so that you don't burn it. Then flip it. Work in batches if needed, making sure the quesadillas do not overlap each other.

Cut into quarters and dip into the Lime Crema!

★ *Makes 4* ★

INGREDIENTS

1 lb. boneless, skinless chicken thighs

Marinade

½ cup chopped cilantro

4 cloves garlic, minced

½ tsp. oregano

1 tsp. chili powder

1 tsp. salt

1 tsp. pepper

1 tsp. onion powder

1 tsp. cumin

⅓ cup olive oil, plus 3 T. for cooking

Lime Crema

8 oz. Mexican Crema

1 lime, zested and juiced

Toppings

1 cup shredded Mexican cheese blend

1 can black beans, drained and rinsed

6 oz. cotija cheese, crumbled

1 purple onion, pickled (page 145)

1 jar of Mama Lil's peppers

8 (6-inch) flour tortillas

HUMILITY AND FOOD

If you find yourself proud and in need of some humbling, might I suggest that the kitchen is always a great place to relearn the discipline of humility? Absolutely everyone fails in different ways in the kitchen. Some of my most recent failures include botching pad thai, ruining BBQ pizza, and thinking I can make J. Kenji López-Alt's General Tso's chicken without looking at the recipe.

I had made pad thai one week and it was perfect. I got too excited the following week and went back to make it again, only this time I thought adding more tamarind paste would increase our enjoyment. Nope. It's true, you can have too much of a good thing.

The BBQ pizza failure was a result of pure laziness. I had made a perfect BBQ pizza and needed to simply slide it off the pizza peel into the pizza oven, but it was stuck. Rather than take the extra ten seconds to hold the peel up to my mouth, pick up the edge of the dough and blow under the crust to lift it (yes, it's a hack that works), I—like an animal—just kept shaking it, hoping it would slide off perfectly, with full knowledge that failure was looming. Yes, it

failed. I ended up with a glob of perfect BBQ pizza in the back of the oven, burnt to a crisp.

The General Tso's fail was also humbling. J. Kenji López-Alt is a culinary genius who resides here in Seattle. His General Tso's chicken is one of the greatest things anyone can make. I make it almost once a week. Because I'm so familiar with the recipe, I thought I was on target. I wasn't. Recipes are your friends.

Failure is something we hate to budget for, and yet, like anything at which we aspire to become great, we must embrace those moments for what they are, learn, make adjustments, and grow. The great Julia Child is commonly quoted as saying, "The only real stumbling block is fear of failure. In cooking you've got to have a what-the-hell attitude." Amen! We have to just go for it, take some risks, and not be so hard on ourselves when we come up short in the kitchen. Jeff Potter, author of *Cooking for Geeks*, turns the question of failure on its head. He asks,

> How much better off would we be if we talked about "success in learning" instead of "failure in the kitchen"? There's not much to learn when things work. When things fail, you have a chance to understand where the boundary conditions are and an opportunity to learn how to do something better next time.[4]

Not only is humility found in the kitchen, but it also comes with the dining experience from time to time. Sometimes the humility comes through not knowing how to get into your crab claws. Other times it comes through not knowing how to pronounce something on the menu. Can you think back to something you used to despise but now crave? For

my wife, Jana, it's oysters. When I graduated with my first post-graduate degree, my dad took us all out for oysters. I was in heaven and Jana was, well, not so much. The waiter brought out trays of all kinds of oysters, and Jana tried one, then she gave me "that look." I don't remember what she ate that night—I suppose it was probably chicken fingers and fries, or maybe the trout. But the creatures in the shell were not something her palate could handle. It was no bother to the rest of us, but it was something that she wanted to like just as we liked it, but it just wasn't there for her. The sight, the texture, everything about the oyster was utterly repulsive. Until one day.

About ten years ago, after my gentle nudging, endless begging, and perhaps a little shaming, she bravely tried again. Fully expecting to be repulsed, she was shocked. This time, it all changed. She fell in love with eating fresh oysters. Now, for surprise dates, she'll take me out for oysters; the buttery, sweet, fruity, acidic finish is her favorite thing, and I'm happy as a clam about it (I know, terrible pun).

Venturing out in dining will require us to be a bit brave, not only in challenging our tastebuds with flavors and new textures but also in recognizing that learning a vocabulary surrounding different cuisines takes time and intentionality. Speak with anyone who works very closely with a particular food, and you'll suddenly notice all kinds of words that are associated with their craft. Sommeliers do not drink wine like the rest of us. They will use words and metaphors that you never thought you'd hear associated with wine. Speak with a butcher or two about why they prefer a particular cut of meat and, again, your vocabulary will broaden. Ask a cheesemonger to explain a few favorites in the case and why. You'll learn something! Remember, "God opposes the proud but gives grace to the humble" (James 4:6). Amen.

Octopus Tacos with Pineapple Salsa

DIRECTIONS

Bring a large pot of water to a simmer, then add the octopus and allow it to simmer for about 40 minutes., adjusting the heat as needed. Remove the octopus from the water and drain. Then use kitchen scissors to remove the tentacles, one at a time. Discard the beak, eyes, and head.

Mix all marinade ingredients, and place the tentacles in the marinade for 2 hours in the refrigerator.

While the octopus is marinating, combine all the ingredients for the salsa in a bowl, mix well, cover, and place it in the refrigerator.

Preheat the grill to 425°. Brush the tentacles with olive oil and sprinkle them all over with salt and pepper. Grill the tentacles for about 3 to 4 minutes per side, flipping once. You'll know they're done by simply pushing a knife into the thickest part of the tentacle. If it goes in easily, it's cooked.

Chop the tentacles into bite-size pieces on a cutting board and then build your tacos. Take a warm tortilla, add some octopus, and finish with a big scoop of salsa.

★ Serves 4 ★

INGREDIENTS

1 (3½ lb.) fresh octopus (if you're in Seattle, you can grab a fresh octopus at Pike Place Market)

Marinade

2 oranges, juiced

1 lemon, juiced

6 garlic cloves, minced

1 pinch red pepper flakes

Olive oil

Salt and pepper, to taste

Salsa

1 fresh pineapple, chopped

1 shallot, finely chopped

1 cup peeled and diced jicama

1 lime, juiced

1 chili pepper, seeded and finely chopped

1 tomato, chopped

1 cup chopped fresh cilantro

2 T. unsweetened coconut flakes

½ tsp. salt, or more to taste

6-inch flour tortillas, warmed or fried (page 135)

6

RESURRECTION:
"Do You Have Anything to Eat?"

On a crystal clear spring Monday morning in Seattle, I stand in my kitchen, barefoot, still wearing a hoodie from the night before—completely unaware he, the King, is on his way. Mindlessly, I begin slicing a tomato as I prepare lunches for the kids to take to school. Luke Howard's "Prelude for a Single Voice" is quietly playing on the record player in the lounge. A chickadee lands on the pale blue flower box on the other side of the window and begins to sing along with her joyous morning song. Suddenly, I'm here, *really* here—aware, more attuned, more present than maybe ever in my entire life. To my surprise, I haven't even had a cup of coffee. As I place the razor-sharp knife on the dull wooden cutting board, I am suddenly gripped by the reality that the same God who walked in the cool of the day with Adam and Eve is here now, walking among pots, pans, knives, and lunch boxes. A simple breath prayer is all that's needed: "Good morning, Lord. Thank you for coming by. I can't believe it's really you."

Brother Lawrence was a seventeenth century priest and writer who gave his life to serving God in the monastery through the humble work done in the kitchen and in repairing other monk's shoes. Suddenly, his words were no longer bound to a page; they, by nothing less than God's grace, had become my own experience: "The time of business does not with me differ from the time of prayer, and in the noise and clatter of my kitchen, while several persons are calling for different things, I possess God in as great tranquility as if I were upon my knees at the Blessed Sacrament."[1]

155

God was with me, on that early morning in my kitchen, in a way that was no different from Sunday morning in worship, receiving communion.

A moment later, our son, Jude, makes his way into the kitchen looking as disheveled as his dad. He playfully bumps into me and shouts, "Look out, old man! It's time for Golden Grahams!" My tranquil moment is gone, and in a way, it is enhanced. Jude's silly way of barging into the kitchen, completely unaware that he is in the presence of God, is just what's needed. As my boy opens the pantry, he discovers the one thing he so longed for in the moment is nowhere to be found: "Paddy! We're out of Golden Grahams! Do we have anything to eat?" Every human being asks that question a few times throughout life. Not even the Lord Jesus himself could escape the same question.

Proof of the Resurrection

The gospel story tells us that after Jesus was arrested the disciples had gone into hiding, knowing that the religious leaders and Roman authorities would show them the same grim ending their leader faced on Good Friday. Yet on Easter Sunday Jesus triumphed over the grave once and for all! He suddenly appeared in the disciples' hideout and reacquainted himself with his friends who had utterly failed him. To their shock, Jesus arrived not as an accuser armed with guilt, shame, and brutal accountability but as a friend, with unbegrudging truth, triumph, and God-sized tenderness. It's hard to imagine a frowning Jesus on Easter Sunday. "But the whole group was startled and frightened, thinking they were seeing a ghost!" (Luke 24:37 NLT). Gently looking the terrified ragamuffins in the eye, he posed two fundamental questions; the first is of the heart, the second is, well, of course, of the stomach.

Jesus asked them plainly, "Why are you frightened? . . . Why are your hearts filled with doubt?" (Luke 24:38 NLT). The disciples were like you and me, people who grow afraid and full of doubt when the joy of life goes down the drain and the dreary gloom of death looms all around. Rather than storming from the room of failed followers, Jesus pursued his troubled disciples because "Love bears all things

... endures all things" (1 Corinthians 13:7). In conviction and kindness, he offered them the opportunity to investigate for themselves what their eyes and ears simply could not believe. People did not rise from the dead back then any more than they do today. So Jesus insisted, "Look at my hands. Look at my feet. You can see that it's really me. Touch me and make sure that I am not a ghost, because ghosts don't have bodies, as you see that I do" (Luke 24:39 NLT). And "as he spoke, he showed them his hands and his feet" but still, they were in disbelief, "filled with joy and wonder" (Luke 24:40-41 NLT). Joyful disbelief is the only emotion I can imagine any of us would have felt had we been there, our jaws dropped open like panting alligators.

Having revealed his heart, adorned with the sweet fragrance of forgiveness, and opened his everlasting arms with heaven's embrace, Jesus then curiously, even humorously, asked one last question: "Do you have anything here to eat?" So "they gave him a piece of broiled fish, and he ate it as they watched" (Luke 24:41-43 NLT). For some, this detail being included may seem strange or irrelevant, but it is actually one of the most important passages in the New Testament. Jesus is found dining in front of his disciples like any other human being! Jesus wasn't like the pirates aboard the *Black Pearl*, eating and drinking only to see the food and wine run right over their bony ribs, through their bodies, and onto the deck of the ship. Jesus was no pirate, he was no ghost; he is the risen King of kings! As he ate, the disciples watched, and their faith suddenly sprung up like never before.

The bodily resurrection of Jesus is the definitive and single most important claim in all of Scripture. Paul writes, "If Christ has not been raised, then our preaching is in vain and your faith is in vain" (1 Corinthians 15:14). Jesus's resurrection sets him apart from every good teacher, prophet, philosopher, and religious figure. There are spiritual giants like Abraham, Moses, and Peter, and there are political powerhouses like Caesar, Napoleon, and all the kings and queens of England, yet Jesus alone towers over humanity as the one who was raised from the dead and will never die again. When he ate fish with the disciples, Christ gave them undeniable proof that he was the same man they had followed for years. They had abandoned him over the weekend, yet he now dined in their midst. This simple proof solidified their faith once and for all.

We also can't lose sight of the truth that what we covered in chapter 4: The dinner table is a table of friendship. The dining experience was as much about affirming friendship as it was about calming a grumbling stomach. Jesus did not berate his disciples for their failures but simply began to eat, signifying that their friendship with him was not lost to shame any more than he was lost to the tomb. Let this be of encouragement to you—Jesus was unashamed to dine even with those who denied him only three days prior. As the sixteenth-century Anglican theologian Richard Sibbes said, "There is more mercy in Christ than there is sin in us."[2] Thanks be to God! Jesus *still* receives sinners and eats with them.

The Kingdom Is Here

Jesus's choice to allow the disciples to inspect his hands, feet, and side and to eat broiled fish gives insight into the coming kingdom of God. It is real. It is physical. And it is going to be *here*. Unfortunately, so many of us in the West have a vision of heaven more influenced by Hollywood and Plato than by what Isaiah and Jesus have to say. In philosophical terms, many have a dualistic approach to their spirituality. It is not uncommon for people to think of heaven as a disembodied state in which our consciences somehow exist in an ongoing posture of meditation, peace, and adoration of God.

Yet both the Old and New Testaments tell us that God is going to usher in "a new heaven and new earth" (Revelation 21:1, also Isaiah 65:17). Hebrews 13:14 says, "Here we have no lasting city, but we seek the city that is to come." Some interpret this verse to teach a form of escapism—that is, this world is useless, and so we should simply wait on God to take us all to heaven somewhere up in the sky. But the Bible is not saying God will throw this whole creation in a landfill somewhere else and make an entirely new creation. Instead we're told that the cities and places we live in *now* will not always be this way. One day there will be no more violence, hunger, or reason to lock our doors. God will renew *this* world, and we look forward to living in that city. Heaven on earth is what the Christian life, both now and then, is all about.

As God one day renews all things, including the physical bodies of the followers of Jesus, we will enjoy eternal life, in bodies that will never see corruption. Our new bodies will be just like the body Jesus has *now*. The Bible paints a picture of wholeness where both our physicality and spirituality will become so integrated and glorified that the whole earth will rejoice and give God glory. This vision not only gives us hope in the resurrection to come but also challenges us and invites us to consider how we view the physical world and people all around us. In the beginning, God originally created and called the world "good." In the end, we will behold him doing the same. In the meantime, consider how this ought to speak to and challenge us to consider our physical world.

QUESTIONS TO CONSIDER

Jesus chose to eat with the disciples to prove he was truly resurrected from the dead. The next time you eat a meal alone, take note of that, and give yourself a moment to reflect on this reality.

Since God is going to renew this physical world, how should this change how we think about our spiritual life and physical life as integrated rather than separated? What would it look like for you to have greater integration of your physical and spiritual life?

Sandwiches and Burgers

Absolutely none of these make the cut in modern, trendy diets, but they more than qualify for cheat days and backyard hangs. The Steak au Poivre sandwich is a famous sandwich that deserves a gold medal. Look through the recipe and think about what ingredients are missing and what else you think might be good to add. Crispy prosciutto, for example?

The Aged Gouda Grilled Cheese is the result of me taking a week back in 2015 and experimenting with about ten different kinds of grilled cheese sandwiches. They were all my favorite, so I just had to pick one to share here.

The Seven in Santa Fe Smash Burgers are in honor of one of the greatest trips of my life with some of my dearest friends: Nate Burke, Don Clark, Dustin Kensrue, Jesse Bryan, Brian MacDonald, and Mike Anderson. Nate lives in Santa Fe. He organized a few days for us to be together with no set agenda. We ate great food, went to art galleries, visited a spa, hiked, and even enjoyed being silent together. We're all so different and yet so similar. Our routines and work were disrupted in the name of playtime. Piling in and out of a minivan, we kings ate whatever we desired. Christmas burritos, chili-cheese burgers, wagyu Hawaiian ribeyes, arguably the best tacos that have ever graced the world, Aztec hot chocolate, and chocolate truffles with flavors of prickly pear, goat cheese and sage, and passion fruit. We hiked out into the desert with the dry earth crunching beneath our feet. We marveled at how the wind and rain and even time herself shaped these rock formations over millions of years. I overheard Dustin telling Nate the definition of a *rill*. He said "it's the tiniest of streams." I sure felt like a rill standing out there in all that space with my friends. Tiny but alive.

Whiskey-Glazed Blue Cheese Smash Burgers

DIRECTIONS

Combine ground beef, garlic, cumin, salt, and pepper in a medium-size bowl and mix well. Form four burger patties by scooping up a handful of the meat mixture and rolling it into a ball—just a bit smaller than a baseball. Set the burgers aside and go make the glaze.

For the glaze, add all ingredients to a small saucepan over low heat. Continue to stir and cook over low heat until all the ingredients are thoroughly blended. Return to the burgers.

Place the burger balls on a cutting board and press your thumb down into the middle of the first burger. Do this for each burger, then heat the vegetable oil in a skillet over medium heat. Place the burgers thumbprint side up in the skillet and allow them to begin to sear. Then turn over and smash each burger, creating a nice edge all the way around. Allow the burgers to cook through, and then top each with 1 tablespoon blue cheese crumbles, cover the pan, and allow the blue cheese to melt (about 2 minutes). Then pull the burgers from the skillet and place them on a paper towel-lined plate to drain.

Place each patty on a brioche bun and top with glaze. If you'd like, you can also add hot sauce and some caramelized onion (page 173) or crispy onions.

★ Serves 4 ★

> **SMASH BURGERS:** Smash burgers are different from traditional burgers. The thumb print technique allows for the more round end to get hot and gain a crispy edge to it. Then flipping and pressing the burger (indention side down) into the pan allows the burger patty to cook evenly.

INGREDIENTS

Burgers

1 lb. 80/20 ground beef

2 T. minced fresh garlic

1 T. ground cumin

1 tsp. pepper

1 tsp. salt

1 T. vegetable oil

4 T. crumbled blue cheese

Whiskey Glaze

¼ cup whiskey (pick what you want to cook with—I'd go cheap on this one, personally)

¼ cup ketchup

½ lemon, juiced

2 T. honey

2 T. low-sodium soy sauce

1 T. liquid smoke

1 tsp. Dijon mustard

1 tsp. Worcestershire sauce

¼ tsp. garlic powder

Serve

Dash hot sauce

4 brioche buns

Seven in Santa Fe
Smash Burgers

DIRECTIONS

Combine the ground beef, garlic, cumin, and pepper in a medium-size bowl and mix well. Make the burger patties by separating the meat mixture into four equally sized portions and rolling each into a ball (just a bit smaller than a baseball). Set the burgers aside, then make the queso.

To make the queso, melt the butter in a skillet on medium high heat and then sauté the onion and garlic for a couple of minutes (but do not overcook) and then turn the heat to very low, sprinkle the all-purpose flour over the onion and garlic, and stir to make a kind of paste. Then add the milk, whisking to blend the ingredients completely. Add the chiles, cumin, salt, and cayenne and continue to whisk. Bring the heat back up to medium high and slowly begin to add the cheese, whisking constantly. When all the cheese is fully melted, remove from the heat.

Return to the burgers. (See note on page 163.) Place the burger balls on a cutting board and press your thumb down into the middle of the first burger. Do this for each burger, then heat the vegetable oil in a skillet over medium heat. Place the burgers thumbprint side up in the skillet and allow them to begin to sear, about 30 seconds per side. Then turn over and smash each burger, creating a nice edge all the way around. Allow the burgers to cook through, then place it on a bun and top with the chile queso. From there, it's all you! I suggest a thick slice of European bacon, lettuce, tomato, crispy fried onions, and Spicy Tangy Mayo (page 147).

★ Serves 4 ★

INGREDIENTS

Burgers

1 lb. 80/20 ground beef

2 T. minced fresh garlic

1 T. ground cumin

1 tsp. pepper

2 T. vegetable oil

Hatch Green Chile Queso

2 T. butter

½ medium white onion, minced

4 garlic cloves, minced

2 T. all-purpose flour

1 cup whole milk (add more milk to thin if desired)

½ cup (4 oz. can) Hatch green chiles, roasted, stemmed, seeded, and chopped

½ tsp. ground cumin

½ tsp. salt

1 pinch cayenne pepper

1 cup shredded Monterey Jack cheese

1 cup shredded cheddar cheese

Serve

4 burger buns

Burger toppings of choice (optional)

Beef Satay Smash Burgers with Thai Peanut Sauce and Lime Cabbage

INGREDIENTS

Lime Cabbage

3 cups finely chopped purple cabbage

1 carrot, shredded

½ cup mayonnaise

1 lime, juiced

1 T. white sugar

¼ cup chopped fresh cilantro

¼ tsp. pepper

Burgers

1 lb. 80/20 ground chuck

2 T. minced fresh garlic

2 T. low-sodium soy sauce

2 tsp. sweet yellow curry powder

1 tsp. Thai fish sauce

2 T. minced fresh ginger

1 T. chopped fresh cilantro

1 tsp. pepper

2 T. vegetable oil

Thai Peanut Sauce (page 121)

Serve

4 burger buns

DIRECTIONS

Make the lime cabbage first. Combine all the ingredients in a bowl, mix them well, then cover and place the bowl in the refrigerator until it is time to eat.

The burgers are next. Combine all the ingredients in a medium-size bowl and mix well. Form the burger patties by separating the meat mixture into 4 equally sized portions and rolling each into a ball (just a bit smaller than a baseball). Cover with a towel and set aside. Make the peanut sauce (page 121).

Return to the burgers. (See note on page 163.) Place the burger balls on a cutting board and press your thumb down into the middle of the first burger. Do this for each burger, then heat the vegetable oil in a skillet over medium heat. Place the burgers thumbprint side up in the skillet and allow them to begin to sear, about 30 seconds per side. Then turn over and smash each burger, creating a nice edge all the way around, and finish cooking.

When the burgers are cooked, place the patties on buns, drizzle on some peanut sauce, and add a scoop of lime cabbage.

★ Serves 4 ★

DINING AND JUSTICE

The apostle James offers some of the most sobering words of rebuke in the New Testament concerning injustice inflicted upon the poor by the rich. There were some belonging to the church in Jerusalem who were guilty of cheating day laborers out of the pay they had earned. James writes, "Behold, the wages of the laborers who mowed your fields, which you kept back by fraud, are crying out against you, and the cries of the harvesters have reached the ears of the Lord of hosts. You have lived on the earth in luxury and in self-indulgence. You have fattened your hearts in a day of slaughter" (James 5:4-5). James warns them that God is just and that there will be a day of accounting for all the evil done to the poor.

What does this have to do with you and me? If you can afford a cookbook such as this, you are among the wealthiest people who have ever lived in human history. Such are the facts. Being as wealthy as we are, we often don't think about things that deserve our attention and appreciation. How often do you think about where your food comes from? I don't mean what you collect at the grocery; I mean who grew the produce? What is their skin color?

Who harvested the wheat? What is their native language? Who caught the fish or slaughtered the cattle or worked long hours in a factory, sorting and processing the goods sitting in your refrigerator right now? Organizations like United Farm Workers (established in 1962) exist to bring to light issues surrounding the injustices in farm labor. What we consistently see is that ethnic minorities are placed in harsh working conditions, oftentimes making the minimal amount of money. Such should never be the case, and yet our fallen world persists.

Jesus calls his followers to an entirely different way of life; we are to embrace being the "salt and light" of the world. In the ancient world, salt was used as a preservative because refrigeration wasn't available to almost anyone. Thus, in calling us to be the "salt," he's saying that we are to be people who aim to preserve the world and fight decay such as injustice. Perhaps you could take some time to reflect on the groceries that you purchase. Are those involved in getting your food from farm to fork compensated fairly? You and I will likely not meet many of these people face-to-face, but we can pray for them, thank God for them, and seek their welfare.

Andy's "Fire in the Hole!" Philly Cheesesteak

I'd like to dedicate this cheesesteak to Andy Maier. One Friday afternoon I was in the mood for some Philly Cheesesteaks. I had enough to share so I texted my friends Kirk Castro and Andy Maier and let them know that the gooey goodness would be on the griddle in thirty minutes. Sure enough, both guys were there in no time, ready to go. Yes, they're married guys with wives and kids and jobs—but somehow they were able to drop whatever it is they were up to and come over. As I grilled the cheesesteaks, Andy played a new track off the upcoming Opponent record (Opponent is a metal band that Andy started). As we scarfed down our cheesesteaks, with drop B metal blaring out the back door, Andy placed a Mama Lil's pepper on the end of his sandwich and said, "Fire in the hole!" It was perfect.

DIRECTIONS

Slice the hoagie rolls about three-quarters of the way through, to make a hinge with the bread to hold the filling.

Preheat a griddle or skillet on the stove over medium high heat. Add 2 tablespoons of olive oil and allow it to heat until it shimmers. Saute the onion first, adding salt and pepper to taste. Then remove the onion and add the steak. It will cook quickly, so keep an eye on it and don't overcook. Then cover the steak with the cheese slices and add a lid to the pan to allow the cheese to melt evenly across the top of the steak. This won't take long!

Uncover the pan, add the onion back in, and mix well. Remove everything from the pan or griddle and put it in a covered bowl to keep warm. Add the last tablespoon of olive oil to the griddle or pan and press the buns into the oil, cut side down, causing them to heat and crisp up just a bit. Remove the bread and fill the rolls with the cheesesteak. And if you want to add just a tiny kick, add a couple of Mama Lil's peppers to the cheesesteak and shout, "Fire in the hole!"

★ Serves 4 ★

INGREDIENTS

4 hoagie rolls

3 T. olive oil, divided

1 yellow onion, thinly sliced

Salt and pepper, to taste

1 lb. sukiyaki-style beef (thinly sliced beef) or thinly sliced rib eye

8 slices provolone cheese

Mama Lil's peppers, to taste

Aged Gouda Grilled Cheese with Sun-Dried Tomato Pesto

DIRECTIONS

Heat the olive oil in a pan and cook the onion, adding a light sprinkling of salt and pepper as they cook. Then add the balsamic vinegar. Cook on low for about 30 minutes to allow onion to caramelize and the vinegar to reduce.

While the onion is caramelizing, make the Sun-Dried Tomato Pesto.

To assemble each sandwich, add cheese to the bottom piece of bread, then pile on some caramelized onion, follow with more gouda, and then add the top piece of bread. Preheat a fresh skillet over medium, melt the butter in the skillet, and grill the sandwiches for about 3 minutes per side.

Serve with Sun-Dried Tomato Pesto in a ramekin on the side for dipping.

★ Serves 2 ★

Sun-Dried Tomato Pesto

This pesto is great on roasted potatoes, garlic naan bread, sandwiches, or even as a flatbread pizza base.

Add all the ingredients except the olive oil to your food processor in the order listed. Begin on low speed, slowly drizzling in the olive oil. Monitor the pesto closely and stop processing when it has reached your desired consistency.

INGREDIENTS

2 T. olive oil

1 sweet onion (sliced)

Salt and pepper, to taste

½ T. balsamic vinegar

8 oz. aged gouda, freshly shredded

4 slices rye bread

1 T. butter, for grilling

Sun-Dried Tomato Pesto

1 (8½ oz.) jar sun-dried tomatoes packed in oil

1 cup fresh basil leaves

1 T. tomato paste

2 T. diced onion

½ cup grated Parmesan cheese

¼ cup pine nuts

3 cloves garlic

¼ tsp. salt

¼ tsp. pepper

½ cup olive oil

THE FOOD SPECTRUM

How we feel about food often depends on where we live and the life stage in which we find ourselves. In the city, for example, there are always new restaurants opening up, hoping to push the limits or challenge the norms, offering urban people the endless opportunity to try new things. On one end of the food spectrum, it can become an obsession, as the temptation to stay completely on top of the food scene is quite fun. For many of us, it would be wise to pay attention to how high our standards may have become. The definition of gluttony might need to be broadened a bit. We often understand gluttony in reference to how much food we eat. Overconsumption is something that we in the West are guilty of more often than not because there really is an abundance all around. Yet we must press further beyond whether we are overeating and simply ask about what we think we are entitled to consume day by day, meal by meal. That is, *is gratitude at the center of our hearts*? Or has greed and entitlement overgrown the center of who we are? Our self-centeredness feeds our attitudes and expectations around what we will and will not eat. If this is pressing a button for you, pause and reflect; ask yourself, "Do I believe that I'm always deserving of something better?" Has food become an idol for you?

On the other end of the food spectrum we find those who are more or less indifferent to what is consumed every single day. People who dwell in this realm tend to see food as fuel and nothing more. It's surprisingly easy to fall into this approach toward what we eat. The truth is, many of us are blessed to be able to easily meet our daily needs, and therefore we buy groceries, cook, or stop in somewhere to eat without much of a thought about the God who provided the food or the hands that harvested and prepared it for us. For those inclined toward indifference, we should challenge ourselves to slow down and give a few moments of thought and prayer to just how much God graciously provides on a daily basis. Thank him for his provision, remembering that he bestows not only groceries for your cupboard but ultimately sustenance that will satisfy your soul.

Jesus famously said, "Man shall not live by bread alone, but by every word that comes from the mouth of God" (Matthew 4:4). In essence, he was saying that the words, will, and ways that proceed from God's mouth are what will provide the human soul and life with the deepest nourishment. Living on God's words provides the remedy for the entitlement and indifference we feel toward all that he provides around the table. Next time you eat, don't just *say* "Grace." Feel it. Taste it.

Slow Cooker Cherry Pulled Pork Sliders with Slaw and Blue Cheese

INGREDIENTS

3 lb. boneless pork shoulder roast

Salt and pepper, to taste

2 T. smoked paprika

1 T. onion powder

1 T. garlic powder

1 T. canola oil

½ cup ketchup

½ cup apple cider vinegar

½ cup brown sugar

2 chipotle peppers packed in adobo sauce

3 T. adobo sauce, from chipotle pepper can

½ cup dried cherries

Lime Cabbage Slaw

½ small head of green cabbage, thinly sliced

¾ cup lime juice

¼ cup white wine vinegar

¼ cup chopped fresh cilantro

1 lime, zested and juiced

2 T. mayonnaise

Serve

Slider buns

Blue cheese, crumbled

DIRECTIONS

Rub salt and pepper all over the pork shoulder and place it in the slow cooker. Then combine the paprika, onion powder, garlic powder, canola oil, ketchup, vinegar, and brown sugar in a bowl, mix it well, then pour it over the pork.

Add the chipotle peppers, adobo sauce, and dried cherries to the slow cooker.

Cook the pork on low for 8 hours. Meanwhile, prepare the slaw (see below).

Shred the pork with two forks. Assemble the sliders: layer the buns with the pork as the base, then top with blue cheese crumbles, and add the slaw.

★ Serves 8 ★

Lime Cabbage Slaw

Mix all ingredients together in a bowl, then cover the bowl and place it in the refrigerator until you are ready to eat.

Classic Steak au Poivre Sandwiches

DIRECTIONS

Season the steaks on both sides with salt. The pepper is where it's *at* on this one! Coarsely grind the peppercorns in a grinder or with mortar and pestle. Take your time, and make sure there's a rough texture. Press the steaks into the peppercorns on one side, trying to cover as much surface area of the steak as possible. Add the vegetable oil to a skillet, and heat on medium-high until shimmering. Add the shallot and cook for 1 minute. Add the mushrooms and garlic and cook for 2 minutes to break down the mushrooms, continuing to stir so as not to overcook the shallots. Stir in the red pepper flakes. Remove the vegetables from the pan and place them in a small bowl, leaving the liquid in the skillet. Reheat the skillet to medium-high heat and place the steaks into the pan, peppercorn side down. Add the brandy, broth, and heavy cream. Spoon the liquid over the steaks continually. Turn the steaks gently, cooking about 3 to 4 minutes per side. When the steaks reach medium rare (135°), remove them from the pan and allow them to sit for 1 minute. Add the mustard to the pan and whisk, then remove from heat.

Slice the steak thinly.

Slice the ciabatta and toast it in the oven at 350° for 2 to 3 minutes.

Spoon the sauce in the pan over the base of the bread, then top with steak, then the vegetable mix, then more sauce, Mama Lil's peppers, and finally some microgreens.

★ Serves 4 ★

INGREDIENTS

2 (10 oz.) New York strip steaks, 1½ inches thick

Salt

3 T. peppercorns

3 T. vegetable oil

½ large shallot, sliced

5 or 6 baby bella mushrooms, sliced

1 garlic clove, minced

1 tsp. red pepper flakes

2 T. brandy

¾ cup low-sodium chicken broth

¾ cup heavy cream

1 tsp. Dijon mustard

Ciabatta bread

Mama Lil's red peppers

½ cup microgreens

SANDWICHES AND BURGERS

7

HOSPITALITY:
Practice What You Eat (Faithful Presence)

If I invite you into my home, I am a host. Only when I also invite you into my heart do I become hospitable. If I care more about the smudge on the wall than the thing on your mind, I miss the point of "us." If I braise the duck to perfection but am distracted by my phone, I am absent. As said earlier, people who are becoming wholly human in Christ do not see those we invite into our homes as supporting actors in the drama of our own lives. They *are* our life! The art of Christian hospitality goes far beyond mere entertainment and dining to our bellies' content. The hospitality in the story of God always begins in the heart and then finds its way to the kitchen and finally to the table. It is about communicating to your guests that they truly *belong*—not just at your table but in this world, and most importantly, they belong to God.

One beautiful example of belonging first to God and then to others is found in the story and writings of Brother Lawrence, who I mentioned in the last chapter. At age twenty-six, the great Brother Lawrence (1614–1691) of Hériménil, France, devoted his life to serving God at the Discalced Carmelite priory in Paris. The monastic life provided the time and space for him to "practice the presence of God," for which the discipline would later be known. He spent his days serving his brothers through the humble tasks of cooking and repairing sandals. For most of us, this sounds like a dreary, burdensome, joyless life, yet Brother Lawrence had a reputation for being surprisingly cheery. His happiness was ever guarded through his diligent practice of remaining present to God even during even the most mundane tasks. He would pray through the day and not wait until sacred hours in worship to finally speak with God. Whether he found himself in the kitchen or receiving communion during mass, he knew that all of his life with God was sacred, not just certain moments. His discipline was to strive to remain in an ongoing conversation with God. After his death, his writings, teachings, and correspondence with others came to be collected and finally published in the now-famous book *The Practice of the Presence of God.*

He said,

> [It is not] needful that we should have great things to do. . . . We can do little things for God; I turn the cake that is frying on the pan for love of him, and that done, if there is nothing else to call me, I prostrate myself in worship before him, who has given me the grace to work; afterward, I rise happier than a king. It is enough for me to pick up but a straw from the ground for the love of God.[1]

Jesus said, "Come to me, all who labor and are heavy laden. . . For my yoke is easy, and my burden is light" (Matthew 11:28, 30). This light-hearted monk took Jesus up on his offer and found himself quite content. The art of remaining faithfully present to God is precisely where hospitality toward others begins. To be truly present to others and serve them well, we must first ground ourselves in the unchanging reality that God is always present with us. Cooking has taught me more about faithful presence than anything else. This is because cooking something *well* requires our attention. Yes, the phone can ring, a child can ask for help, the dog may need to be let out, but the reality is that you can't stay gone for long. You must *show up!* Again, a life well lived is a life that is truly present to God, self, and others.

> Cooking requires that we be fully present. This is one of its greatest teachings. It keeps bringing us back to what is happening in the moment and continually calls our attention to what we are doing. We smell when the cake is ready to come out of the oven and we taste when the soup is almost done to perfection. When the water boils on the stove, we turn down the heat.[2]

Christian hospitality is about practicing the presence of God *with others in your home*. The world out there can be cold, dark, sharp, and entirely indifferent to the things that keep us up at night. Our souls ache, our minds race, and our hearts break as we are assailed by plagues of time, sudden traumas, or plain monotony. The hospitality of God is the reprieve every human being longs for, whether we know it or not, and it is often best felt through the lives of those willing to love, serve, and listen. Though invaluable, the comforts of food, drink, and conversation around the table are short-lived. Therefore, Paul instructs us to make "the best use of the time, because the days are evil" (Ephesians 5:16).

Be Faithfully, Wholly Present

Time is ticking by ever so quickly. As we come together, we can't afford to pass the time the way we thoughtlessly take out the trash or doom-scroll on our phones. We must make it a point to really show up. "Be attentive to time and the way you spend it. Nothing is more precious. This is evident when you recall that in one tiny moment, heaven may be gained or lost. God, the master of time, never gives the future. He gives only the present, moment by moment."[3]

This doesn't mean everyone who comes into your home owes you their entire life story, including all the skeletons in their closet. What it means is that as you spend time together, you're doing the faithful work of *listening*. "Listening is the way we are present to time, to self, to another, to God. Listening is not something you can do in retrospect—it is not remembering; listening is the way we attend to here and now in the fullness of time."[4] As a pastor, I have the tremendous honor of meeting with people throughout the week; sometimes, I have answers people need, and other times I don't. I know that people desperately long to be heard. We live in a noisy world, and often, people don't share their wins or losses simply because so many are just not listening.

What if, in the name of practicing faithful presence to others, the church first offered a listening ear to the world around us? Rather than leading off with our "airtight" arguments for God's existence and what he wants of us, we would offer the world our genuine friendship. Could it be that the church is often viewed as dated, archaic, and entirely irrelevant to society because of our unwillingness to listen to others, our tendency to remain inhospitable? As a result, fewer and fewer people are finding any reason to convert and be associated with the church. This isn't because the gospel cannot withstand intellectual scrutiny; more often than not, it's because Christians are consistently guilty of retreating and sequestering ourselves off from the world that God so loves (John 3:16).

Hospitality: The Strongest Apologetic for the Gospel

Perhaps the most robust defense of the truth and trustworthiness of the gospel is not our clever thoughts, not our sound, reasonable defenses for the resurrection, but our willingness to practice hospitality as Christ did, our commitment to hear others fully. We are often quick to speak and slow to listen, yet to practice hospitality in the way that Jesus and the early church did, we must resolve to truly *hear* others; when people are heard, people are healed.

Yes, there's a time and a place for sermons in churches and lectures in classrooms, for books to be read and information to be discussed. Yet the deep things of God and humanity require that we come to the table seeking both to know and be known. Jesus's way of hospitality has far more to do with the heart of the host than the presentation of a charcuterie board, proper plating, and table settings. Maya Angelou is often attributed with saying, "People will forget what you said, people will forget what you did, but people will never forget how you made them feel." Christian hospitality cares not only about the gospel's truth but also the tone with which it is shared.

As Brennan Manning says, "To evangelize a person is to say to him or her: you, too, are loved by God in the Lord Jesus. And not only to say it but to really think it and relate it to the man or woman so they can sense it. This is what it means to announce the Good News."[5]

As Jesus ascended to the right hand of God and sent the Holy Spirit into the church, he launched a campaign, a vision not only for non-personal creation but for all of humanity: we can now live as whole human beings. Yet, as we see throughout Scripture, the kingdom of God appears to us as upside down. What I mean by "upside down" is this: God consistently works in ways that baffle each of us because his thoughts are not our thoughts, and his ways are not ours. We need to realize that as high as the heavens are above the earth, so are his thoughts above our own (see Isaiah 55:8-9).

In the Old Testament, God chose the nation of Israel to be his covenant partner, not because she stood out among the nations but precisely because she was so easy to overlook. Upside down. God chose Moses, a stuttering murderer on the run, to lead in the liberation of the Hebrew slaves and give the law to the people. Upside down. God chose David, the weakest of the brothers, to be anointed as the strong king of Israel. Upside down.

Over in the New Testament, we see the great reversals continuing. A woman giving two pennies is considered more generous than the millionaire writing big checks. Why? Because she gave out of lack rather than plenty. Turning the other cheek is a tremendous virtue—mercy triumphs over revenge. God prefers to find the particularly weak things in the world to overcome what most consider "strong."

Reading about the birth of Christianity in the book of Acts, we find that the church was not born into luxury, convenience, and ease. Many Jews and Romans were anything but hospitable to the young, vulnerable church. Christians were—as many still are around the world today—violently persecuted. So how on earth did Christianity spread like wildfire all over the Roman Empire? Was it their clever arguments, picket signs, and bumper stickers? Perhaps it was their professional production teams and fashionable preachers, their rock bands and building campaigns? Could it have been that they held all the political power? Was it because the Christians belonged to a superior class or caste system that afforded them the best education and accommodations? No. It was none of these things!

Everything can be traced back to what Jesus said at the Last Supper: "By this all people will know that you are my disciples, if you have love for one another" (John 13:35). The love of God, expressed through the hospitable hearts and homes of Christians, continues to be infinitely stronger than the sword, prison bars, and social ostracism. The reckless love of God has always been the strength of the church.

As we close this chapter, we must consider that living out what it means to be wholly human and practicing faithful presence to others through Christian hospitality will cost more than groceries and time. Ultimately, we will feel the cost of God loving the world through us at an emotional and relational level. Loving our neighbors as ourselves is as costly as it gets.

C.S. Lewis said that "to love at all is to be vulnerable. Love anything, and your heart will certainly be wrung and possibly be broken."[6] Practicing the way of Jesus and extending true hospitality to a weary world means that we're willing to roll up our sleeves and become present to the people, the stories, and the needs around us. Love is costly. It takes time to really get to know someone. More than that, the emotional cost of presence is high, because when someone knows they truly belong, they can open up—they can share their real stories, pains, griefs, and losses. Yes, hospitality will certainly cost you more than groceries; it will cost some tears as well. Such is the nature of the healing kingdom of God.

How can you leverage your kitchen as a place to encounter God in the way Brother Lawrence did?

What would it look like to budget for the practice of hospitality not only but also relationally? What can you do to prepare yourself to love someone in a costly way?

Pasta and Pizza

This may sound crazy to you—it certainly sounds crazy to my friends—but I never really cared for pizza until I turned 40. It's now one of the things I am most commonly tempted to make. (I know. Terrible. Blame Jana. It's her fault. I already have confessed that I'm a sinner and in need of grace, so just bear with me.)

Pizza was never really my favorite thing growing up. Maybe it was all the pizza blasts at church and soccer parties? I don't know, really. I'm sure that the combo of square pizza, corn, and chocolate milk served in public school didn't help either. During my vegetarian days when I was just out of high school and in my early college years, I really enjoyed—and *still love* (no shame!)—Papa John's Veggie Pizza. In fact, when Jana and I started dating, one of our favorite things to do on rainy days was to order veggie pizza and binge *Star Wars*. So pizza wasn't totally out of the picture, but you get the idea.

Everything changed on the twenty-fifth evening of May in the year of our Lord 2020, when I turned 40.

My friend Joel Cummings brought over his portable Ooni pizza oven, freshly acquired from a Kickstarter campaign, along with dough and all the toppings for me and just a few of my buddies. He made us pizzas for hours! With each pizza, I fell more and more in love. It was like scales were falling off my eyes like Saint Paul himself, and I was actually *seeing*, for the first time in my life, just how wonderful pizza really is. Jana bought me an Ooni and I've been hooked ever since. In fact, I can think of about a dozen friends who have gone on to purchase Ooni pizza ovens as a result of my influence.

Some of us are slower than others. But again, grace is for guys like me.

Marinara Sauce

This is great for margherita pizza, shakshuka starter, and arancini dipping sauce starter.

DIRECTIONS

Sauté the onion and garlic in olive oil on medium-high heat. Add salt and pepper and red pepper flakes after the onion and garlic have begun to break down a little bit. Then turn the heat to low and hand crush the tomatoes into the pot and stir in the tomato paste. Taste the sauce, and add more salt and pepper if needed.

Let the sauce simmer for 20 minutes, then turn off the heat and allow it to begin to cool just a bit. If desired, pour the marinara into a blender or food processor, and blend it, monitoring the sauce until it reaches your desired texture (some people like it chunky; others like it far more thin).

★ *Makes 1 quart* ★

INGREDIENTS

3 T. olive oil

1 medium white onion, thinly sliced

2 T. minced garlic

1 tsp. salt

1 tsp. pepper

1 big pinch red pepper flakes, or more to taste

1 (28 oz.) can whole peeled San Marzano tomatoes

3 to 4 T. tomato paste

NOTE: This sauce is so versatile, you might want to make a bigger batch and use it as a starter for other recipes. If you're making shakshuka (page 31), simply sauté the bell peppers in the shakshuka recipe with a little olive oil, then stir in this sauce, along with the paprika and cumin, as listed. Follow along the rest of the recipe from the eggs forward.

If making a dipping sauce for something like arancini, simply add more red pepper flakes to get to your desired heat level, and puree it a little longer than you might for a pizza or pasta sauce.

Pizza Dough

My beloved mother, Bevy, got me a KitchenAid stand mixer a couple of years ago, which is great for mixing and kneading dough. However, I put my time in doing all of this by hand for two years before she came to my rescue. Moms will do anything for their kids, won't they?

Double zero flour, or 00 flour, is the classic finely ground Italian flour for making pizza dough. That is preferred for this recipe, but you can also use bread flour.

DIRECTIONS

Add the water to the bowl of a stand mixer fitted with the dough hook. Then add the yeast and allow it to sit for five minutes. Add the flour and salt and mix on low speed for 7 to 8 minutes. You may need to add a pinch of flour occasionally to help the dough thicken up just a bit. Stay patient and don't rush the process. You can burn out an engine! As the mixer works the dough, the dough should start pulling away from the sides of the bowl and forming into a clump. When it's a nice, soft dough clump, pull it out, and fold it into a ball. Dust the dough ball with a bit more flour and allow it to rise for at least 90 minutes, covered with a cloth.

When it's time to start making pizzas, sprinkle some flour on a large flat surface (a kitchen counter will do just fine). Break the dough into five equally sized dough balls. Put one ball of dough in front of you, and press down with the palm of your hand into the center, creating the initial shape of a pizza: a low, flat center with edges to it. Then begin stretching it out. There are multiple techniques for this! Have a look around online and find one that works for you. I prefer the "steering wheel" method, in which you hold the dough out in front of you like a steering wheel and allow it to stretch while you turn it clockwise. Feel free to use a rolling pin as well.

Once you have your dough stretched to the desired size, it's time to make pizza. Use your conventional oven or make it out on your Ooni or the like!

★ Serves 5 ★

INGREDIENTS

2 cups warm water

1 tsp. quick-rising yeast

4 cups 00 flour, or bread flour, plus more for kneading and rolling dough

1 T. salt

Flour, for sprinkling

Margherita Pizza

INGREDIENTS

Pizza dough, uncooked (page 193)

Marinara sauce (page 191)

Fresh mozzarella log or ball, cubed

Fresh basil

Salt flakes

Quality olive oil, such as DeLaurenti Sicilian Riserva EVOO

DIRECTIONS

Preheat your oven: set a conventional oven to 425°, or as advised by the manufacturer if you have a backyard pizza oven (about 750°). Roll or stretch the dough to the desired size on a flat surface. Evenly spread a few tablespoons of marinara on the dough. Distribute about 8 to 10 pieces of mozzarella somewhat evenly atop the sauce, and off to the oven you go! If you're using an Ooni or another pizza oven, this should take only about 1 to 2 minutes to cook. If you're cooking with a conventional oven, bake it on a pizza stone for about 20 minutes.

When the pizza is done, allow it to stand for about 3 to 4 minutes. Then add basil and a few salt flakes, and lightly drizzle a nice olive oil over the top.

★ Serves 5 ★

Pepperoni Pizza

DIRECTIONS

To make a classic pepperoni pizza, follow the recipes for pizza dough and marinara sauce. Preheat your oven: set a conventional oven to 425°, or as advised by the manufacturer if you have a backyard pizza oven (about 750°).

On a flat surface, roll or stretch the dough to the desired size and number of pizzas. Evenly spread a few tablespoons of marinara on the dough, then add a handful of cheese. Sprinkle oregano over the cheese, then layer on the pepperoni.

If you're using an Ooni or another pizza oven, this should take only about 1 to 2 minutes to cook. If you're cooking with a conventional oven, bake it on a pizza stone for about 20 minutes.

When the pizza is done, allow it to stand for about 3 to 4 minutes.

★ Serves 5 ★

INGREDIENTS

Pizza dough, uncooked (page 193)

Marinara sauce (page 191)

12 oz. mozzarella cheese, grated

1 tsp. fresh oregano, chopped

2 cups sliced pepperoni

PASTA AND PIZZA

KIDS IN THE KITCHEN

For those graced with children, whether biologically or through adoption or foster care, inviting them into the sacred space of the kitchen is a fantastic way to spend time together while also teaching them a few things. Discovering this was really good news for me because I am absolutely the world's worst handyman. I wish it were different, but it is what it is: I'm useless with the traditional tools you find in your garage. Fortunately, I have several friends who kindly take me under their wings and lend me a hand with working on my house, car, or motorcycle. So while I'm not so gifted in one space, I can pass on the knowledge and a few skills that I've picked up over the years in the kitchen, and so I do! How to care for kitchen tools and keep a clean workspace while prepping dinner are transferable skills that will set my kids up for what they'll be doing all their lives—cooking, hosting, and dining right!

The age of a child obviously determines how much time you can spend together in the kitchen. Really small ones may only have the attention span to handle some take-and-bake cookies, which involves preheating the oven, opening the packaging, greasing a baking sheet, evenly spacing the cookies on the baking sheet, baking them, and then allowing them to cool for a couple minutes as you pour milk and pick out a book to read or choose a cartoon to watch while you enjoy this sweet and simple treat with your child.

For children who are a bit older, you can try out some more time-consuming recipes, though it helps to set the child's expectations first. *News flash:* Your preteen might not appreciate being suddenly pulled away from friends for a four-hour lasagna-making marathon without a warning that this is an all-day commitment. If you know you've got a rainy Saturday coming up with nothing on the calendar, you could invite your kids to spend an afternoon with you in the kitchen. Perhaps they get to pick the appetizer, main course, or dessert? My children and I have other activities and experiences we share together—Daddy dates to arcades, going out for bubble tea and ramen, soccer practice, shooting hoops in the cul-de-sac, walking with our dog, Dempsey—but I've found that cooking with my kids is particularly effective in giving us something to do while we're able to also talk about life. They're currently thirteen and eleven years old; they're learning, thinking about, and wrestling through all kinds of things every single day, whether it's something they observed in the city, a conversation they've recently had with a friend, or a question about their faith. The conversations tend to flow a little easier while our hands are busy and we can break up our chats with simple requests like "Hey, could you please turn that burner down?" or "Will you get me two egg whites?"

Beyond spending invaluable time together, you really are teaching them skills and techniques they will pass on to their children—your grandchildren—not so many days from now. All is grace.

BBQ Chicken Pizza

INGREDIENTS

Pizza dough, uncooked (page 193)

2 boneless, skinless chicken breasts, (about 1 lb.)

½ tsp. salt

½ tsp. pepper

Fresh mozzarella log or ball, cubed

Mama Lil's peppers

1 cup chopped fresh cilantro

BBQ Sauce

1 cup vinegar

¼ cup ketchup

1½ T. brown sugar

3 tsp. yellow mustard

1 tsp. pepper

1 tsp. celery seed

1 pinch red pepper flakes

DIRECTIONS

Sprinkle both sides of the chicken evenly with salt and pepper and then drizzle both sides with olive oil. Then head to the charcoal grill. (See "Tips for Grilling Chicken" on page 121.) Keep a close eye on the chicken breasts so as not to over- or undercook them. Once they're fully cooked (after about 10 minutes), remove the chicken from the grill, place it on a cutting board, and chop it into smaller cubes.

Preheat your conventional oven to 425° degrees or a pizza oven to approximately 750°.

Roll out the pizza dough, drizzle a couple tablespoons of BBQ sauce onto the dough, and spread it around with the back of a spoon or a spatula. Then add the cooked chicken, cubes of mozzarella, and a few Mama Lil's peppers. Bake your pizza: about 20 minutes on a pizza stone if using a conventional oven or 1 to 2 minutes in a pizza oven. Top with fresh cilantro just before serving.

★ Serves 5 ★

BBQ Sauce

No, this isn't my granddad's recipe. It'll never happen. Don't ask. I wish I could share. But here's something that will get close to that which belongs only to the Early home. I'm sorry, but a promise is a promise.

In a saucepan, whisk all the ingredients together over low heat for 10 minutes. Allow it to bubble just a little and then allow it to cool.

Chicken Ragù with Goat Cheese and Red Swiss Chard

In this recipe you have to be prepared to move fast! Read through the recipe before you begin, and be sure to prepare all your ingredients and have all your cooking tools handy before you start. There is a lot of multi-tasking, but if you have everything ready to go, you'll be fine.

DIRECTIONS

Place the chicken thighs on a plate, pat them dry, and sprinkle salt and pepper on both sides. Drizzle them with olive oil. Add 3 to 4 tablespoons of olive oil to a braiser and turn to medium-high heat. Once the pan is preheated, add the chicken and brown both sides *without* cooking the chicken all the way through, about 4 minutes per side.

While the chicken is browning, start boiling a large pot of water for the Swiss chard.

Pull the chicken from the pan and set it on a plate, covered. Turn down the heat to medium, add the onion and garlic to the pan, and allow it to cook in the remaining oil and chicken fat. Sprinkle it with salt and pepper and add a pinch or two of red pepper flakes. Cook for about 7 minutes.

Add the pancetta and brown, about 2 minutes.

Separate the leaves from the stalks of the chard. Discard the stalks, and boil the leaves for 2 minutes. Using tongs, remove the chard from the pot, place it in a strainer in the sink to drain, then submerge the chard in a bowl of ice water.

Add the fusilli to the pot of boiling water and cook it to al dente, according to package directions. When the chard is cold, slice it up thinly and add it to the caramelizing vegetables.

Hand crush the tomatoes into the braiser, adding the remaining sauce from the can. Stir well, then add the tomato paste and stir, followed by the red wine.

Chop the chicken to the desired size and add it to the sauce to finish cooking. Taste the sauce and add more salt and pepper if needed.

Drain the cooked fusilli and then add it to the braiser, stirring thoroughly.

Let the ragù simmer for about 15 minutes more, stirring occasionally and adjusting the heat as needed. Do a final taste-test, add salt, pepper, or red pepper flakes if needed, then remove the pan from the heat.

When you're ready to eat, crumble the goat cheese into the braiser, stirring it in well and allowing it to melt thoroughly throughout the dish.

Serve in warmed bowls with a crispy baguette and a nice zinfandel.

★ Serves 4 ★

INGREDIENTS

5 to 6 boneless chicken thighs (you can also make this with the skin on, but the kids aren't fans so I go skinless)

Salt and pepper, to taste

4 to 6 T. olive oil, divided

1 purple onion, thinly sliced

4 to 5 garlic cloves, thinly sliced

¼ to 1 tsp. red pepper flakes

4 oz. pancetta, diced

1 large bunch red Swiss chard

½ lb. fusilli pasta

1 (28 oz.) can Mutti whole peeled tomatoes

4 T. Cento Double Concentrated Tomato Paste, or more to taste

½ cup red wine (I use Chianti)

4 oz. goat cheese

Sausage Ragù

This comes to us from Julia Moskin of *New York Times* Cooking website, who originally adapted it from renowned Italian pasta chefs Sara Jenkins and Nancy Harmon Jenkins. It's floated around the internet pasta world since about 2015 and I'm putting my version into print right here! This is a dish that you need to budget just a little extra time for because it takes a bit for the veggies to caramelize in the sausage. I, alongside a few of my buddies, have tried to take a shortcut and caramelize the veggies separately to save time. Don't do it! It's not worth it and doesn't even come close. Brown the meat, then add the veggies, and allow the magic to happen! The deviations I've made here include mixing the sausages to add some heat. Also, when serving, I've found that adding cheese to the steaming pasta in a bowl for just a moment and letting it melt, then adding the ragù, and then more cheese and parsley is the way to go.

DIRECTIONS

Heat a heavy skillet or Dutch oven and over medium-low heat. Remove any sausage casings, and crumble the meat into the pan. If there is not much fat in the meat, you may need to add a little olive oil as you stir and break up any sausage chunks. Cook only about 5 minutes until the meat is opaque but not browned.

Stir in the onion, carrot, celery, and parsley. Add a little olive oil if needed, and turn the heat down to very low. Cook the vegetables with the meat, stirring often, until the vegetables begin to caramelize and the meat is brown. This may take as long as 40 minutes, but this slow cooking is very important for the flavor of the dish.

Use your hands to break up the tomatoes and add them to the meat mixture. Stir, and pour in any additional juice from the can. Increase the heat a tad and bring the sauce to a simmer, then add the herbs and simmer, uncovered, for about 20 minutes or so. You're looking for a thick sauce with almost all the liquid absorbed.

Meanwhile, start a large pot of salted water on the stove to boil the pasta. While the next step is happening, boil your pasta according to package directions, to al dente but do not drain. Time the cooking of the pasta to finish at the same time as the cooking of the ragù sauce.

Mix the tomato paste with the hot water, then add this to the pan, reduce the heat again to very low, and keep cooking for about 10 more minutes until the sauce is a beautiful, smooth, deep red color. Remove the herb sprigs. Sprinkle black pepper over the ragù, stir, and taste.

When the pasta is cooked, place about 2 cups of the cooking water in a large serving bowl to heat the bowl up a little, then drain the pasta. Return the noodles to the pot over low heat. Stir about a cup of ragù into the noodles, along with a bit of the reserved cooking water. Stir well and cook for another minute or two until the noodles are cooked to your preference, adding a little more ragù or water if needed.

Drain the water from the serving dish, add the pasta, and sprinkle liberally with parmesan cheese. Allow the cheese to melt into the pasta for a minute or so, then ladle the ragù over the noodles, sprinkle with additional chopped parsley, and serve hot with additional Parmesan cheese.

★ Serves 6 to 8 ★

INGREDIENTS

½ lb. hot Italian sausage

½ lb. sweet Italian sausage

Extra-virgin olive oil (optional)

1 onion, minced

1 carrot, minced

1 rib celery, minced

¼ cup minced flat-leaf parsley, plus extra for garnish

1 (28 oz.) can whole tomatoes, preferably San Marzano, with juice

1 large sprig fresh thyme

1 large sprig fresh rosemary

3 T. tomato paste

1 cup hot water

Salt and pepper, to taste

1 lb. penne noodles

Parmesan cheese, freshly grated (optional)

Bucatini all'Amatriciana

This dish is literally hundreds of years old and is as good as ever!

DIRECTIONS

Heat the olive oil in a large saucepan on medium-high heat. Add the guanciale and cook until brown. Add the red pepper flakes and white wine, then hand crush all the tomatoes into the saucepan. Add salt and pepper to taste.

Then boil a pot of salted water and cook the bucatini until nearly al dente.

Meanwhile, preheat your oven to 140° degrees. Place oven-safe bowls into the oven and allow them to heat up for about 10 minutes.

Just before the pasta reaches al dente, turn off the heat on the pasta pot and use your tongs to transfer the noodles straight into the tomato sauce. Stir in the pecorino well, then add ¼ cup of the hot pasta water.

Serve pasta in the warmed bowls, straight out of the oven, and top with extra cheese.

★ Serves 4 ★

INGREDIENTS

1 T. extra-virgin olive oil

6 ounces guanciale, cut into very small squares (if you can't get your hands on guanciale, pancetta also works nicely)

Pinch red pepper flakes

¼ cup dry white wine

1 (28 oz.) can whole peeled tomatoes

Kosher salt and freshly ground black pepper, to taste

1 lb. dried bucatini pasta

1 oz. grated Pecorino Romano cheese, plus more for serving

8

Wedding Supper with the Lamb

Living in London changed our lives. After college and my first master's degree were complete, I was offered a position to study at the London School of Theology. A dream come true! I enrolled in another master's program and engaged in aspects of biblical interpretation (also known as the field of hermeneutics). My classmates were from all over the world: Colombia, Iceland, the Congo, the Faroe Islands (a country I'd never even heard of!), China, Vietnam, Austria, and so on. Literally everywhere. Studying Scripture in that diverse context was more than humbling. These brilliant men and women taught me so much. The creative questions they would ask and the unique perspectives they offered from their own cultural backgrounds were unlike anything I'd ever come across. In fact, it wasn't just their academic brilliance but the ways in which they looked at the world. They saw many things so differently from how I naturally saw things as an "American"—and by "American" I mean *North American*. Yes, on day one, we were in a seminar, going around the room introducing ourselves, stating our names, our previous degrees earned, and, of course, where we were from. When it was my turn, I said I was from "America." Daniel, a classmate from Brazil, looked a little puzzled and then, with a playful tone, said, "Which America? Did you know there's another one to the south?" I blushed, and everyone laughed, especially me, as I said, "Oh boy! I've got a lot to learn!"

I received another gift one Friday afternoon. Our class had just completed a seminar session discussing ancient Babylonian texts. Chloe, a woman from Singapore with an interest in Old Testament metaphors and human imagination, asked me a question on the sidewalk. "Alex, this is unrelated to class, but could I ask you a question about why Christians from your part of the world often feel like they need to do 'big things' for God? Why all the mega churches and music and lights and all that?" I was taken back a bit and really didn't have a good answer. I bumbled out, "Well, I suppose it's because the Bible tells us to go into all the world and make disciples of all nations, and things like that." She said, "Oh, I see. That's interesting. In Singapore we had a saying growing up: 'If you can walk down the beach and leave no footprints, that is a life well lived.'" I had that dog-that-heard-a-whistle confused look on my face. She continued, "What it means is that living a life that doesn't call attention to oneself is really special. We tend to gravitate toward Paul's sayings like 'work quietly with your own hands.'"

I'll never forget that gray afternoon on the sidewalk. What a gift those days were. Since returning to the United States and watching so much unfold over the years in regard to racism, violence, and all types of injustice, I often think back to my classmates in London with a profound appreciation for the ways they challenged me to see the world. More than that, they challenged me to long for the world that is still to come.

Whispers of What Is to Come

The dark shadows of sadness, pain, and death were cast over all creation as Adam and Eve ate the forbidden fruit under the serpent's deception and gave way to God-denying, stomach-worshiping rebellion. The snake slithered into the garden and conned God's children, and everything has been groaning and longing for paradise ever since. But as we've seen, all is not lost! No, the kingdom of God has broken in already. And one day those dark shadows will flee once and for all under the light of what St. John of the Apocalypse calls the wedding supper of the Lamb. Because of God's grace, mercy, and provisions, what began in rebellion will find its crescendo in reconciliation, singing, dancing, and heart-swelling jubilee! John writes,

> Then I heard what seemed to be the voice of a great multitude . . . crying out, "Hallelujah! For the Lord our God the Almighty reigns. Let us rejoice and exult and give him the glory, for the marriage of the Lamb has come, and his Bride has made herself ready; it was granted her to clothe herself with fine linen, bright and pure"—for the fine linen is the righteous deeds of the saints. And the angel said to me, "Write this: Blessed are those who are invited to the marriage supper of the Lamb" (Revelation 19:6-9).

Yes! Raise your glass and shout with your friends and family, "To the King!"

As you come to the wedding supper of the Lamb, I implore you, please come with *biblical* expectations and let us leave our short-sighted, often homogenous ways of life out of the picture entirely. The room will be packed and as eclectic as creation itself! The King's smile will fill us with more joyous ecstasy than ten thousand days in any earthly paradise we've ever dreamt of seeing.

> After this I looked, and behold, a great multitude that no one could number, from every nation, from all tribes and peoples and languages, standing before the throne and before the Lamb, clothed in white robes, with palm branches in their hands, and crying out with a loud voice, "Salvation belongs to our God who sits on the throne, and to the Lamb!" (Revelation 7:9-10).

I don't suppose anyone can come close to grasping the beauty that John saw at that moment. Today, over seven thousand known languages are spoken worldwide, yet everyone will be understood at this dining table. There won't be a weapon in sight, because they will have beaten "their swords into plowshares and their spears into pruning hooks" (Isaiah 2:4). There will not be one racial slur, side-eye, or secret judgment of the heart at the multiethnic dining table of the King of kings.

Every last one of us who has lost our way, our faith, our friends, our appetite, and even our own minds will suddenly have our wits about us like never before. As far as the eye can see in each direction, men and women caught up in the global history of the grace of Almighty God will be clothed in fine linen (see Revelation 19:8). Afros, mohawks, long hair, short hair, dreadlocks, braids, and colors of all kinds will be a glory unseen this side of heaven. It's not hard to imagine someone nearby singing the classic song, "I Can See Clearly Now." It truly will be a bright sunshiny day!

That day is so good, so glorious, so impossibly wonderful that it *has* to be true. What John beheld is the often unsaid, unexpressed, unimaginable longings of every human heart. Each setback, tear-drop, and funeral causes the soul to yearn for the hope that is heaven. Deep within us all, down in our bones, we crave the marrow of life. It is what the Bible calls "shalom," and that is precisely what we are destined to taste and see at the wedding supper of the Lamb.

Yale University's Nicholas Wolterstorff, famed professor of theology and philosophy, gives a comprehensive definition: "Shalom incorporates *delight* in one's relationships. To dwell in shalom is to find delight in living rightly before God, to find delight in living rightly in one's physical surroundings, to find delight in living rightly with one's fellow human beings, and to find delight even in living rightly with oneself."[1] Shalom cannot be had in isolation; instead, the Biblical model of shalom always considers the people and place in which life is lived and how life is life. To practice shalom in the here and now, we must agree with the conviction of Dr. Martin Luther King; we truly *need* one another. In the Christmas Eve sermon he gave at the Ebenezer Baptist Church in 1967, Dr. King said,

> Did you ever stop to think that you can't leave for your job in the morning without being dependent on most of the world? . . . You reach for a bar of soap, and that's given to you at the hands of a Frenchman. And then you go into the kitchen to drink your coffee for the morning, and that's poured into your cup by a South American . . . Before you finish eating breakfast in the morning,

you've depended on more than half of the world. . . We aren't going to have peace on earth until we recognize this basic fact of the interrelated structure of all of reality.[2]

We truly need one another. As a society, we are constantly confronted by the insufferable racism in the human heart, which consistently manifests itself in fear, rejection, injustice, violence, shame, and countless deaths. Throughout the ages, the church, no doubt, has often inexcusably participated in the blatant embrace of thought patterns, beliefs, and behaviors belonging to the world that remains at enmity with God. So those complicit in the wrongdoing are rightly critiqued and called to account for the sins of hypocrisy and cold indifference demonstrated toward the world we say Jesus loves. As the apostle John put it, "If we say we have fellowship with him while we walk in darkness, we lie and do not practice the truth" (1 John 1:6).

From the pages of the New Testament, down throughout the Middle Ages, and up through the antebellum South, there have been professing Christians of every tribe and tongue that have fallen grossly short of the command of God to "love your neighbor as yourself" (Leviticus 19:18)—or, even better rendered, "Love your neighbor *for he is like you.*" Instead, many have foolishly chosen to march to the beat of the evil one rather than follow in the footsteps of the peace-making Messiah, and the results are always the same.

A grave sin that has plagued the church for thousands of years is the notion that one can love Jesus personally and yet withhold the love of neighbor by remaining indifferent toward justice. For those who profess to follow Jesus, it would be wise to remember the time he condemned the Pharisees by mentioning the *spice rack* and justice in the same sentence. He said, "But woe to you Pharisees! For you tithe mint and rue and every herb, and neglect justice and the love of God. These you ought to have done, without neglecting the others" (Luke 11:42). Jesus is always interested in us becoming whole human beings, a transformation that calls us to go beyond tedious religious observance and into the realm of seeking justice on behalf of others. Unfortunately, the church has fallen short—and always will. She will continue to have sin to repent of and places to grow. Yet we can rejoice in this: she is the bride of Christ and won't always be this way. She will one day be *glorified*!

The apostle Paul says, "Christ loved the church and gave himself up for her, that he might sanctify her, having cleansed her by the washing of water with the word, so that he might present the church to himself in splendor, without spot or wrinkle or any such thing, that she might be holy and without blemish" (Ephesians 5:26-27). At the wedding supper of the Lamb, the church will *finally* be without spot or blemish! As Jesus is united with her throughout the ages, she will shine in the glory of God, never to be tempted toward sin again. Racism, prejudice, fear, violence, and indifference toward one another will be cast into hell, never to haunt us again. Scripture doesn't tell us much about what we will be eating. Still, given that Jesus is the host, we might well assume that he plans on accommodating his multiethnic family with the most spectacular home-cooked meal we will ever taste. Dumplings, pasta, and tacos, oh my! (A man can dream, can't he?)

Jesus mentioned this great banquet on more than one occasion—it was on his mind then, and based on what he said, it's safe to bet it's on his mind now. Though his work is finished, there still remains a yearning within him that has yet to be fully realized. Eugene Peterson beautifully renders the words of Jesus found in the twelfth chapter of Luke's Gospel:

> Keep your shirts on; keep the lights on! Be like house servants waiting for their master to come back from his honeymoon, awake and ready to open the door when he arrives and knocks. Lucky the servants whom the master finds on watch! He'll put on an apron, sit them at the table, and serve them a meal, sharing his wedding feast with them. It doesn't matter what time of the night he arrives; they're awake—and so blessed! (Luke 12:35-38 MSG).

After all that he has done for us, Jesus is looking forward to assuming the role of a banquet host. He will take down the apron, tie it around his waist, and prepare a feast fit for a King but given to the servants instead. Beloved, if this is not grace, I don't suppose I'll ever know what is.

Hours before he would be stripped naked, beaten beyond recognition, crowned with thorns, and nailed to the wood of the cross, Jesus picked up a cup of wine. Then, with God's love pounding, surging, and soaring through his heart, he looked his ragtag disciples in the eyes and said, from the depth of his being, "I tell you I will not drink again of this fruit of the vine until that day when I drink it new with you in my Father's kingdom" (Matthew 26:29). Jesus Christ hasn't touched a drop of wine in two thousand years. Still, at his wedding feast, he will raise his cup, and the glorious church made up of people from every nation under heaven will shout throughout the ages, "To the King! To the King! To the King!"

Notes

INTRODUCTION

[1] Frederick Buechner, *Beyond Words: Daily Readings in the ABC's of Faith* (New York: HarperCollins, 2004), 139.

[2] James V. Schall, *On the Unseriousness of Human Affairs: Teaching, Writing, Playing, Believing, Lecturing, Philosophizing, Singing, Dancing* (Washington, D.C.: Regnery Gateway, 2001), 106.

[3] Amanda Ruggeri, "How Mobile Phones Have Changed Our Brains," *BBC* (website), May 18, 2023, https://www.bbc.com/future/article/20230403-how-cellphones-have-changed-our-brains.

[4] Tish Harrison Warren, *Liturgy of the Ordinary* (Downers Grove, Illinois: InterVarsity Press, 2016), 33-34.

CHAPTER 1

[1] These words are spoken during our eucharist experience at church: see Matthew 26:26-28 and 1 Corinthians 11:23-25.

[2] Craig A. Evans, *Jesus and His World: The Archaeological Evidence* (Louisville: Westminster John Knox Press, 2012), 13.

RECIPES INTRODUCTION

[1] Robert Capon, *The Supper of the Lamb* (New York: Farrar, Straus, and Giroux, 1989), 5.

CHAPTER 2

[1] See John S. Allen, *The Omnivorous Mind: Our Evolving Relationship with Food* (Cambridge, MA: Harvard University Press, 2012). See also John S. Allen, "Food and Memory," *Harvard University Press* (blog), May 18, 2012, https://harvardpress.typepad.com/hup_publicity/2012/05/food-and-memory-john-allen.html.

[2] Eugene Peterson, *Tell It Slant: A Conversation on the Language of Jesus in His Stories and Prayers* (Grand Rapids, MI: Eerdmans, 2008), 82.

CHAPTER 3

[1] Matthew 14:13-31; Mark 6:30-44; Luke 9:10-17; John 6:1-14.

[2] Brennan Manning, *Ruthless Trust: The Ragamuffin's Path to God* (San Francisco: HarperCollins, 2009), 169.

CHAPTER 4

[1] S.S. Bartchy, "Table Fellowship," in *Dictionary of Jesus and the Gospels* (Downers Grove, Illinois: InterVarsity Press, 2013), 796.

[2] Brennan Manning, *All Is Grace: A Ragamuffin Memoir* (Colorado Springs: David C Cook, 2011), 107.

CHAPTER 5

[1] Shauna Niequist, *Bread and Wine: A Love Letter to Life Around the Table with Recipes* (Grand Rapids: Zondervan, 2020), 112.

[2] C.S. Lewis, *Mere Christianity* (New York: HarperCollins, 1952), 199.

[3] Rachel Premack, "Why So Many Men Are Cooking," *Washington Post*, July 19, 2016, https://www.washingtonpost.com/news/wonk/wp/2016/07/19/why-so-many-millennial-men-are-cooking/.

[4] Jeff Potter, *Cooking for Geeks: Real Science, Great Cooks, and Good Food* (Sebastopol, CA: O'Reilly Media, 2010), 15.

CHAPTER 6

[1] Brother Lawrence, *The Practice of the Presence of God: with Spiritual Maxims* (Ada, Michigan: Revell, 1967), 12.

[2] Richard Sibbes, *The Bruised Reed and Smoking Flax* (London: S. Rothwell, 1821), 14.

CHAPTER 7

[1] Brother Lawrence, *The Practice of the Presence of God*, 61.

[2] Bettina Vitell, *A Taste of Heaven and Earth: A Zen Approach to Cooking and Eating with 150 Satisfying Recipes* (New York: Harper Perennial, 1993), 68.

[3] "The Cloud of Unknowing," in *The Essential Writings of Christian Mysticism*, ed. Bernard McGinn (New York: The Modern Library, 2006), 264.

[4] Keith Anderson, *Reading Your Life's Story: An Invitation to Spiritual Mentoring* (Downers Grove, Illinois: InterVarsity Press, 2016), 130.

[5] Brennan Manning, *The Ragamuffin Gospel: Good News for the Bedraggled, Beat-Up, and Burnt Out* (Colorado Springs: Multnomah Books, 2005), 124.

[6] C.S. Lewis, *The Four Loves* (London: Harcourt Brace Jovanovich, 1991), 147.

CHAPTER 8

[1] Nicholas Wolterstorff, *Educating for Shalom: Essays on Christian Higher Education* (Grand Rapids, Michigan: William B. Eerdmans Publishing Company, 2004), 23.

[2] Martin Luther King Jr., *A Testament of Hope* (San Francisco: HarperCollins, 1986), 254.

Index

Favorite specialty ingredients

DeLaurenti Sicilian riserva extra-virgin olive oil

Don Chilio jalapeño chili crisp

Fran's raspberry sauce

Gustarosso canned tomatoes

Heartbeat Hot Sauce by Heatonist

Huy Fong Foods sriracha

Inna Jam plenty spicy jalapeño jam

KariKari garlic chili crisp

Kewpie Japanese mayonnaise

Laoganma chili crisp

Mama Lil's red peppers

OMG! vanilla fig barrel-aged balsamic vinegar

Stonewall kitchen red pepper jelly

Acknowledgments

I really mean it when I say, "all of my wealth is in my relationships," and so a section like this could easily just be another book. Fortunately, I have a big table around which I can gather those who would grace my life with the sacred gift of *friendship*. Jon Snell, a fellow ragamuffin, who got me into cooking, is the one who showed me how to enjoy every element of the cooking experience—from the grocery, to prep work, until it's time to call it a night. His oldest friend, Grandy Streets, has graciously shared with me a couple things that appear in this cookbook, and I really hope to dine with him in this age and the age to come. One of the most fun weeks I ever had includes my lifelong friend, Mikey Law. In a previous life he was lecturing at St. Andrews, and we challenged each other to invent a new taco recipe every day for a week straight and report back across the globe. I salute you, Big Homie. Pastor Leonce Crump will undoubtedly FaceTime me anytime he is making gumbo. We'll shift gears from humor, to leadership, to joy, to tears, and never miss a beat. That's relational gumbo! Don Clark, (of Invisible Creature), doesn't do much work in the kitchen. He's an artist who works out of a very cool barn with a perfect orange door, and he is *overwhelmingly* gifted with creative direction and design; he is why this book *looks* so amazing. His thought and careful attention to detail is why he gets to work with some of the world's biggest companies. Words run out when I think about how grateful I am for his humor (I nearly passed out laughing at a text exchange I had with him while trying to write this!), generosity, brilliance, and friendship.

I'm a bit of an odd duck in the sense that I am a trained theologian who serves the Church full time and I have been given the incredibly humbling opportunity to write. Therefore, I serve our church Sunday to Thursday and then reserve Fridays to write. During this season, I enjoyed riding the light rail train here in Seattle downtown to Westlake and then walking over to the famous Pike Place Market. I did all of my writing in a little non-profit library and reading room known as Folio. This beautiful little space is tucked away in the top corner of the atrium and my friends Tess and Caroline were kind enough to keep the break room stocked with La Croix and were always willing to give me a writing break by way of telling me about whatever is going on in their lives. The Pike Place Market is a precious place with honestly the best people in the world. Chaz at Frank's Quality Produce is hands down the most inviting and present human being you'll meet in the market. The cheesemongers at DeLaurenti are the most knowledgeable people on the planet when it comes to cheeses and antipasti. In fact, it is in this beloved place that I discovered the greatest canned tomatoes this side of heaven, Gustarosso. Matt's in the Market restaurant has never served a bad dish and their wait staff is second to none. Storyville Coffee baristas go above and beyond not only by timely and kind service but they even bring warm chocolate cake around and give it out to whoever may want a little treat. And my friends at Place Pigalle (a little French bistro) who, in my opinion, hung the moon.

Lastly, my friends at Town & Country Market—friends I see every single day. Thank you . . . thank you . . . thank you.

Alex Early and his wife, Jana, are happy parents to Tovah and Jude. Alex is a pastor, an author, and a lecturer. Longing for a creative outlet that wouldn't take him away from his family, he found his way into the kitchen—a somewhat surprising place where he has discovered the holy ground upon which relationships flourish. He and his family live in Seattle.